Alcohol Lied to Me: The Intelligent Escape From Alcohol Addiction

2014 - Updated Third Edition

By Craig Beck

Published by Viral Success Limited 2003-2014

www.craigbeck.com

www.StopDrinkingExpert.com

Alcohol Lied to Me

Copyright Viral Success Limited

Paperback ISBN: 978-1-291-03190-4
eBook ISBN: 978-1-291-03185-0

Hypnosis reprogramming tracks mentioned in this book are available to download from
www.stopdrinkingexpert.com

Chapters

1. Introduction

2. Do you have a problem with alcohol?

3. Denial is a problem

4. Where is the power

5. You are not alone

6. Alcohol, our favorite drug

7. Lie down with dogs

8. Threshold moments

9. Deconstructing the addiction

10. The cost of drinking

11. Correcting the imbalance

12. Controlling the ego

13. Dealing with the kick

14. FSQ (Frequently Slurred Questions)

15. Subconscious reprogramming

Introduction

Craig Beck is a well-regarded family man with two children, a lovely home and a successful media career; a director of several companies, and at one time the trustee of a large children's charity, Craig was a successful and functioning professional man in spite of a 'two bottles of wine a night' drinking habit. For 20 years, he struggled with problem drinking, all the time refusing to label himself an alcoholic because he did not think he met the stereotypical image that the word portrayed.

He tried numerous ways to cut down; attempting 'dry months', banning himself from drinking spirits, only drinking at the weekend and on special occasions (and found that it is astonishing how even the smallest of occasions can suddenly become 'special').

All these 'will-power' based attempts to stop drinking failed (exactly as they were destined to do). Slowly he discovered the truth about alcohol addiction, and one by one, all the lies he had previously believed started to fall apart. For the first time, he noticed that he genuinely did not want to drink anymore. In this book, he will lead you though the same remarkable process.

The Craig Beck method is unique...
• No need to declare yourself an alcoholic.
• A permanent cure, not a lifetime struggle.
• No group meetings or expensive rehab.

- No humiliation, no pain and 100% no 'will-power' required.
- Treats the source of the problem, not the symptoms.

Alcohol Lied to Me has already helped thousands of people to escape from alcohol addiction. It has been translated into several different languages and has topped bestseller charts around the world. Newly updated, this third edition of the book includes two new chapters.

Craig also offers personal support and a series of unique tool to help you stop drinking alcohol in his online club – which has helped many thousands of people to quit and stay quit:
www.stopdrinkingexpert.com

Chapter One

Do you have a problem with alcohol?

Most people pick up this book with that 'do I have a problem?' question on their mind. Some are hoping this book will allow them to conclude that they are doing nothing wrong and now conveniently have some written evidence to back up and endorse the continuation of their habit. Others are aware that they are no longer in control and want help to stop drinking and to then stay quit. Stopping drinking, as we all know, is the easy bit. Staying off the booze permanently is the real problem.

So let's answer that initial burning question... do you really have a problem with alcohol?

Yes, but there is not actually anyone who drinks alcohol that doesn't have a problem. Alcohol is in itself a problem and not a solution (as many believe it to be). Therefore if this substance is in your life 'in any form' you cannot help but have a problem. As you will discover in this book, alcohol is an addictive toxin packaged into attractive bottles, marketed with billions of dollars of advertising and so deeply ingrained in popular culture that we can no longer see it for what it really is.

One thing you will quickly discover is that people get very upset when you criticize this drug, they don't even like you referring to it as a drug! Your alcohol-drinking friends would tell me to stop being so melodramatic. They will probably argue that many millions of people around the world manage to enjoy alcohol responsibly and it doesn't negatively affect their lives in the slightest. Some might go further to suggest that for some the occasional drink actually improves or enhances their life. However, this counter argument to my opening gambit only holds water if you suspend the reality that alcohol is actually a poison created from the by-product of decaying vegetable waste.

This book is all about opening your eyes to what is going on behind the smoke and mirrors of alcohol. In truth, alcohol is a poison! So with that fact in mind how can anyone argue that the habitual consumption of a poison is a positive thing? This is difficult to take on board initially because we are conditioned to see alcohol, not as a poison but merely a harmless social pleasantry. So for the sake of argument let's replace the poison used in this argument with a different toxin, hydrogen cyanide for example. Imagine how illogical it would be to try and defend the consumption of cyanide!

Would you say that someone who only consumes cyanide infrequently was a social user or normal user of the chemical? Yet, this is exactly what we do with alcohol. Of course your first response to this will probably be an objection to the comparison. Many will complain that cyanide will kills you stone dead, whereas alcohol just makes you merry. It is true that neat cyanide will kill you but then so will 100% pure alcohol. Heavily diluted cyanide won't kill you but it will make you very ill... are we really a million miles away as comparisons go?

Once you become aware that the emperor isn't actually wearing any clothes at all, and realize that alcohol is none of the things the marketing suggests it is, only then can you start to deconstruct some of the popular language surrounding its use. We talk of these 'normal' and 'social drinkers', the people who can consume alcohol at parties and social occasions but don't appear to be dependent on it to remain functional. Of course, even the most hardened alcoholic at some point was what we would describe as a 'social drinker'; before the mousetrap of alcoholism snapped closed on them, they were considered just as normal as the next guy. The poor problem drinkers looked at them and wondered why they couldn't drink for fun, just like them.

And so the cycle of addiction continues; social drinkers slowly become alcohol dependent problem drinkers, and instantly in the eyes of society they stop being 'normal' and become weak willed, pitifully sad people who, for some reason, can't consume an addictive toxin and stay in control of it. Alcohol is many things, but it certainly is none of the glitzy life enhancing things we are told by the advertising agencies or collectively endorsed lies that have been handed down from generation to generation.

We believe that booze makes a party go with a swing, and yet the next day we happily use words of destruction to describe what a great time we had. We stare out from blood shot eyes, with a tongue feeling like a butcher's chopping block, and gleefully report that last night we were 'trashed, slaughtered, mashed, hammered, destroyed, wasted' or a hundred other different terrible adjectives that now apparently mean something good happened.

The marketing for alcohol would have you believe that simply drinking their specific brand of attractively packaged poison will turn you into the next Brad Pitt or Elle MacPherson. In reality, we know how good a drunk actually looks to us when we are sober. Whether they are male or female there is perhaps nothing less attractive than having someone come up to you stinking of booze, slurring a badly thought out chat up line, as a little bit of saliva drips from the corner of their mouth. Forget the advertising spiel, the only way you can get you more sex while on alcohol is to find someone who is as equally as drunk as you.

Does it really make you a sex symbol if you have to use a drug to get the opposite sex to sleep with you?

The more you think about what you are doing, the more ridiculous it appears. We create lots of distractions to avoid the truth about this drug. We claim it is essential to a good party, we think it makes food taste better and we connect it to social standing. You must surely have heard that if you can afford to pay astronomical amounts of money for your alcohol that makes you a connoisseur, and a person who appreciates the finer things in life (not an alcoholic). Listen to a 'wine expert' talk about the latest vintage to come out of the Bordeaux region and you would think they were describing bottled sex. They talk of a seductive nose and a robust body with a hint of dark chocolate and wild berries. As you will discover in this book, it's all-just the ego creating illusions of grandeur to cover up a bad habit that it would rather you keep up (because it feels nice, or rather it stops an unpleasant sensation of self-induced pain). Intelligent and wealthy people have simply found a way to put a veil of acceptability and snobbery over a common drug addiction.

Back when I was a drinker, I too got trapped into this illusion of finery and alcohol going hand in hand. I allowed myself to believe that the ritual of carefully selecting a very expensive bottle of wine out of my temperature controlled wine cellar, decanting the precious liquid into an exquisite crystal jug, before holding the glass aloft to admire the deep color and rich aroma from the wine meant that I wasn't a problem drinker; I was an expert admiring a piece of art. Some of this 'art' would cost me in the region of $500 a bottle.

Yes, we might have had to forego the annual family vacation to save money, but not surprisingly my cellar was never forced to endure such austerity measures. My wine cellar was apparently never short of cash, even in the toughest times. Such was the depth of my delusion and how strange that those expensive bottles of art were bought with the intention to 'show off' to friends with, and yet they were actually normally opened after a bad day at work, sitting alone as I tried to convince myself that I deserved the liquid gold I was consuming. Daddy was not to be disturbed my wife would tell the children as they were stopped in their tracks on route to excitedly tell me about their day at school. I was just another druggy lying to myself in my basement. I would take a noisy slurp of the fine vintage, drawing the air over the liquid on my palette, and write detailed tasting notes in my journal. Oh yes, I was a connoisseur of the highest order, I could hold my own with even the most seasoned of wine critics.

One Friday evening, I took my wife Denise out to a fine French restaurant as a treat (of course she was driving, she always was), and as we walked into the elegantly lit restaurant, the wine Semillon recognized me, his face lit up with a beaming smile. Walking over to us, he warmly greeted me and shook my hand, asking how I was and how the family was doing. He no more than nodded a welcome in my wife's direction before ushering us to the best table in the house. Before we had a chance to sit he told me that he had just that week taken delivery of the 2003 Chateaux Pontet Canet, it was simply divine he assured me as he walked off to get a bottle.

Denise glanced at the wine list; this particular vintage was $350.00 a bottle. She gave me one of 'those looks' that perfectly encapsulated her feelings about the matter, words were not necessary. I knew she was thinking the kids need new school uniforms and here you are considering blowing it all on one bottle of wine. When the wine waiter returned and proudly presented the label of the bottle to me, I explained it was a little too expensive. He nodded a non-judgmental smile but shot my wife a disapproving glance. He knew I was an easy sale, but there was an irritating voice of reason present who had spoilt it. He recommended a cheaper but still expensive alternative and poured us each a glass while we enjoyed our appetizers.

When our glasses reached a slurp or two away from empty, he returned with several more wide-bodied glasses, each with an inch or so of dark colored, full-bodied red wine pre-poured into them. He placed them all down in front of me, and to my surprise and my that wife's disgust, he pulled up a chair to join us. He sat to my side with his back to Denise; reaching across the table to push the first glass towards me.

"I would value your opinion Mr Beck, these are on the house, just tell me what you think", he said with a huge smile. If he could see the expression on the face of my wife, I doubt he would have been so cheerful!

I should have seen that this guy had hi-jacked what should have been a romantic candlelit meal. In reality I had never planned it as such; it was just another evening activity that I could do that didn't interfere with my drinking. I could just have easily taken my wife to the theatre, but then I would have only been able to drink before the show and during the interval. A restaurant with alcohol on tap was a much better option, and besides, it was too late, my ego had already kicked in; I was flattered to be considered such an expert that this experienced wine waiter would value my opinion so highly. I felt about as significant as you can get, my ego was at pleasure level ten. I picked up the vast glass, cupped it in the palm of my hand and began the performance us wine aficionados like to give when consuming our favorite drug. I slurped loudly, rolled my tongue around, inspected the color against the candlelight and declared my verdict. "Bravo!" he cheered, almost giddy with excitement at my approval. Another glass was pushed forward, and another, and another, until a full thirty minutes had passed by. I don't know how much spectacularly expensive wine I consumed gratis that night, but my, what a splendid evening I thought it to be.

I got home elated (and drunk), crowing about the extraordinary service and attention we had received all evening. My wife frowned at me and walked up the stairs to bed. She didn't say anything about the evening until the next time I suggested we go to the same restaurant.

Her memory of the previous visit seemed to be in direct contrast with my own. She talked of the rude and unprofessional waiter who had ignored her all night and hogged my attention by boring her to death by droning on and on about his wine cellar. The scene she was describing shocked me, it was so far removed from what I had experienced, I even considered that she had maybe been there on a different occasion with someone else. I was much more willing to consider my wife was having an affair than that she didn't enjoy all the free booze we got that night.

Of course, her memories of the night were not clouded by vast qualities of a mind-altering drug. She was right, and I was just another problem drinker who had found a smoke screen to cover my habit that actually worked. I was drinking one or two bottles of expensive, attractively packaged poison a night, but had managed to delude myself that there was nothing wrong in that. I couldn't have a problem because I was clearly a cut above the alcoholic in the park who chugged back super-strength tins of beer. I was buying and drinking the stuff of kings, this was an indication of my social standing and refined palette, and surely not a proclamation of a drug addiction!

Bullshit! Whether your smoke screen is the same as mine or you have managed to create another entirely different one, it's still just bullshit and nothing more. The sooner you grow up and admit this, the better. It doesn't matter whether you drink cheap plonk or expensive wine, it's all the same thing. Alcohol kills just as many intelligent and wealthy people as it does poor and deprived, it doesn't care how much you spent on your habit. The doctor won't cut you open one day and declare you to have the correct type of liver failure and thank goodness you drank the posh stuff and not that horrible cheap cider.

Let me quote you what the world heath organization says about your drug of choice, and then let me ask you if at any point they refer to the type or quality of the alcohol being consumed:

The harmful use of alcohol is a global problem that compromises both individual and social development. It results in 2.5 million deaths each year. Alcohol is the world's third largest risk factor for premature mortality, disability and loss of health; it is the leading risk factor in the Western Pacific and the Americas and the second largest in Europe. Alcohol is associated with many serious social and developmental issues, including violence, child neglect and abuse, and absenteeism in the workplace. It also causes harm far beyond the physical and psychological health of the drinker. It harms the well-being and health of people around the drinker. An intoxicated person can harm others or put them at risk of traffic accidents or violent behavior, or negatively affect co-workers, relatives, friends or strangers. Thus, the impact of the harmful use of alcohol reaches deep into society.

Stop deluding yourself that you are part of something greater, or a member of a special elite club. A bottle of wine a night makes you no better than the homeless person swigging supermarket own label whiskey in the park. Your bottle may have a pretty label, but inside the poison remains the same.

You might assume that cigarette smoking is the world's biggest killer and you would be correct. However, that fact is only true when you apply it to the full spectrum of social demographics. Low paid, manual workers and the elite with their expensive Cubans and the such add a disproportionate number to that figure. Actually when you consider the middle-income earners, then alcohol becomes the true grim reaper.

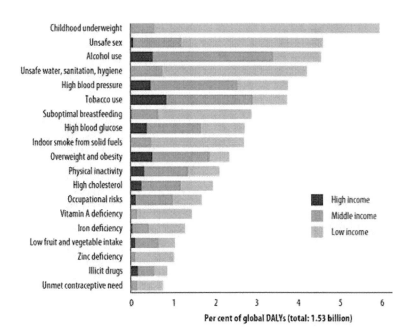

Per cent of global DALYs (total: 1.53 billion)

One of my favorite arguments to prove I was doing nothing wrong was to state loudly and proudly 'hey at least I don't smoke'. I would say this because I felt it proved that I could be doing something much worse – of course along with all the other lies I believed it was just alcoholic smoke and mirrors.

Alcohol is known as the silent killer because so many assume that they would be able to recognize the signs of a problem early enough to simply stop. The fact that they

26

even consider this illogical nonsense as a safety net is evidence in itself that the mousetrap has already been primed. It's exactly the same as the mouse assuming he would have enough time to avoid the steel trap bar and its deadly spike before it got chance to hit him.

With the problem drinker, this one assumption is the mother of all mistakes, because the organ most at risk of fatal damage from alcohol is the liver. This unique part of the body is a piece of natural engineering that way surpasses the label 'genius'. This one organ is responsible for hundreds of vital functions in the healthy human body. So important is it, that it even has the ability to repair itself and can even continue to function with up to seventy percent of its surface area damaged. Now you might think, why would anyone continue drinking if they had already done that much damage to their liver?

The problem is, the liver has very few nerve endings in it, and so you are simply unaware of the damage being caused by the alcohol. Only when the organ itself becomes so swollen from the abuse that it begins to press on other more sensitive areas of the abdomen do addicts begin to feel something wrong and start to worry they have caused some damage.

As I am sure you can appreciate; when a human organ is so badly swollen that it is pressing on other parts of the body with enough pressure to cause pain, it must be in a pretty shocking state. Sadly, it is often only at this point that people think about going to the doctor, but often will put if off as long as possible for fear that (god forbid) the doctor insists that they stop drinking. Often by the time they reach the point where they can't sleep for the pain and can't avoid the GP any longer do they go and get the tests. Many, at this point find out that the damage is irreversible and the only option is a liver transplant.

So you get a liver transplant and everything is fine again, right?

Wrong! There are currently 18,000 people in the United States awaiting a liver transplant. Where do you think you would rank on the waiting list next to the child who was perhaps born with a defective liver, or the woman seriously injured in an automobile wreck. Health services around the world don't look too kindly on people like you who had a perfectly good liver and opted to destroy it. Plus, they make the assumption that you will only go on to abuse the donor organ too, and so you may never see the top of that waiting list.

So subtle is the drug that most problem drinkers are not aware of the precise moment that control was lost and they became alcohol dependent. There certainly is no point trying to work out when you changed from being a 'social' drinker of poison to an addicted drinker of poison.

The only fair assumption to make is that anyone who starts drinking alcohol socially inadvertently primes the mousetrap the moment they take their first sip. Some people will be destroyed by the mechanism and others may never feel the harm, but the only true way to ensure you don't get squashed is to never try and grab that cheese and stay well away from the trap in the first place.

Everyone who drinks alcohol is in the cycle. All those strangers, friends and colleagues you wrongly assume are somehow better than you because they apparently can take or leave a drink are still all mice sitting blissfully unaware of the danger. The steel bar may snap closed on them next week, next year, in ten years time or maybe they will sit there for a lifetime. The only constant is, as long as they continue to consume the addictive drug alcohol, they continue to play a very dangerous game of booze buckaroo™, and you have seen what happens when that mule eventually kicks!

Society insists that there is a profound difference between the people who drink a few bottles of wine a week, and a person who drinks to excess on a daily basis. The latter are described as suffering from an illness called alcoholism; they are labeled as alcoholics and forced by well-meaning support groups to identify themselves by the same derogatory nametag. They are told that they have a condition that is incurable and must for the rest of their life describe themselves as a 'recovering alcoholic'. Perhaps this bleak and depressing ritual explains why 95% of people who turn to organizations such as Alcoholics Anonymous fail to stop drinking. This book is certainly not here to do down the efforts of this organization, or any other method, because for the 5% of people who do escape from the loop using the Big Book theory of alcohol cessation, the rewards are truly life changing.

The reason AA doesn't work for most people is because it requires its members to use 'will-power' to quit. This is the default weapon for human beings when they identify something in their life that is not serving them. From trying to lose weight to giving up an addictive drug we always assume the best course of action is to force ourselves to stay away from the thing we crave. The very idea of 'will-power' is an oxymoron, there is actually no power at all in 'will-power' and later I will explain more about this.

Drinking alcohol is akin to juggling with fire sticks, there is a decent chance you will get burned. The difference in this comparison is you wouldn't then label the people who got injured by the flame as incurable 'fireaholics'. We would be more likely to say that they unfortunately got hurt, as the result of playing with a substance that used in the wrong context is dangerous. Using fire for anything other than cooking and heating is not a safe activity (exactly why we scold our children for playing with matches). Using alcohol for anything other than its chemically defined uses as a disinfectant, germicide or fuel is asking for trouble. Yet, when trouble inevitably arrives with this use of this drug, we choose to blame the person and not the substance that actually caused the damage.

You are not an alcoholic, nor are you weak willed or suffering from an addictive personality. You are none of those things, over 80% of the western world consumes alcohol, and 80% of those people are no longer in control. If you watch the glamour adverts for the latest designer vodka in high rotation across our television screens, you may find that hard to believe. Alcohol appears to be, if not the reason for the party in the first place, the life and soul of its success. Alcohol is potentially the most dangerous and deceptive drug on planet earth! Over dramatic? As we progress on this journey together, I will explain why this is the case.

Let me tell you here and now, you are most certainly not alone, thousands and thousands of people just like you lose control of alcohol every day. That one little drink to help them unwind at the end of a busy day, or the quick pint with friends has turned from a 'like to have' to a 'must have'. As with all drink related problems, this doesn't happen overnight, you don't wake up one morning an 'alcoholic'. These problems develop slowly over 5 to 20 years, so slowly you don't even see them coming. Such is the viciously deceptive nature of this drug that initially there are no negative symptoms to indicate the beginning of a serious problem. As a matter of fact, for most people the beginning of a long battle with alcohol will appear to be woven with an array of positives. Early stage problem drinkers may feel lively, confident and carefree when they drink. Eventually they become known for being 'able to handle their booze', as though this is a positive trait to be proud of. Often these people are described as party animals or the life and soul of any occasion. So while the chemical is working on your brain, your friends and colleagues are working on your ego, a powerful combination indeed.

Many people buy this book not to stop drinking, but rather with the goal of proving to themselves, or even to the caring family members or friends who have questioned their drinking, that they don't have a problem with alcohol. I can sugar coat this next section for you if you wish, I could spend several chapters building up to it, but lets cut to the chase and you can decide whether you want to disagree before we go any further together. Let me fire some questions at you:

• Have you ever planned your day based on the availability of alcohol?

• Have you ever made rules for yourself about your drinking, e.g. I will only drink beer and no hard spirits?

• Has anyone ever questioned you about your drinking?

• Have you ever tried to stop or cut down your drinking and failed before?

A YES to any of those questions my friend, means you have a problem with alcohol. I deliberately don't call you an alcoholic because I know your automatic conditioned response is to defend yourself in the face of such an assault on your perception of who you are. Regardless of how blatant the problem and symptoms appear to be, if you label someone an alcoholic you will quickly get sold the line 'I admit I drink too much but I am most certainly not an alcoholic'. I understand this objection because despite the fact that I consumed on average over 120 units of alcohol a week, and for a period of nearly ten years I still refused to declare myself to be an alcoholic. To this day I point blank refuse to accept that label; I do not believe any of the thousands of people who have stopped drinking via this method are either. You are no more alcoholic than an individual who is constantly scratching his head could be said to be a 'scratchaholic'. Alcohol misuse is the symptom of a problem and not the actual problem itself.

Many people think of alcoholics as disheveled, homeless winos who have lost everything, but there are people who meet the criteria for a medical diagnosis for alcohol dependence who are highly functional in society and still have their jobs, homes and families. This type of drinker is known as a functional alcoholic (or functional problem drinker, whatever label you want to apply). They rarely miss work and other obligations because of their drinking, although it does happen occasionally. They usually excel at their jobs and careers. Typically, they are knowledgeable and witty individuals who are successful in many areas of their lives. To all but those who are closest to them, they give the outward appearance of being perfectly normal.

I know who these people are because I used to be one. I kept my drinking hidden through some of the most successful periods of my career in broadcasting. If you also have a problem with this drug that is currently kept hidden away from your colleagues and family. In this book, I will show you how to take control of the situation without anyone needing to know you ever had a problem in the first place.

Chapter Two

Denial is a problem and not just a river in Egypt!
One of the main reasons that alcoholics seek help for
their drinking problems is the eventual negative
consequence of their alcohol consumption. When the
pain or embarrassment gets bad enough, they can no
longer deny that their drinking needs to be addressed.
For the functional alcoholic, the denial runs deep,
because they have yet to encounter outward negative
consequences to their habit.

They go to work every day. They haven't suffered
financially. Most have never been arrested or on the
wrong side of the law. From their point of view they
simply can't have a problem because they don't fit their
own definition of what a person with a drinking problem
should look like! Don't blame television, Hollywood or it's
actors, they are compelled to keep portraying alcoholics
as the staggering, slurring down and outs that we are
familiar with. If a director instructed his leading man to

play an alcoholic character as a functional alcoholic, how would we even know he had any sort of addiction problem?

The functional problem drinker often consumes just as much alcohol as any fully blown alcoholic; they just don't exhibit the outward symptoms of dependence. This is because they have developed a tolerance for alcohol to the point that it takes so much more for them to feel the effects. Consequently, they must drink increasingly larger amounts to get the high they crave. This slow build-up of alcohol tolerance means the functional alcoholic is drinking at dangerous levels, which can result in alcohol-related organ damage, cognitive impairment and alcohol dependence. Chronic heavy drinkers can display a functional tolerance to the point that they show few obvious signs of intoxication, even at high blood alcohol concentrations, which in others would be incapacitating.

In the mid 90's, Steve McFadden, a popular British soap opera actor, was arrested and charged with driving under the influence of alcohol. He had consumed nine double vodkas before getting behind the wheel of his car. While to most people this would be enough to knock them out for the night, he decided to fight the prosecution on the grounds that he had an unusually high tolerance to alcohol. The courts witnessed the bizarre scene of a man consuming such a vast amount of drink and still appearing to be completely sober. The judge obviously bought the argument as the actor was banned for just 18 months, a very light sentence for such a large blood alcohol reading.

You need to change what alcoholic means to you, it doesn't mean you must accept being a social outcast or that the condition is permanent. Alcoholism isn't a figment of your imagination, and I will keep confirming for you that you are not weak willed or in any way a failure because of this problem. A statement which frequently predicts the response, 'how come I can't just open a bottle of wine and have one glass with my meal?' or 'why can't I ever just have one, like my friends appear to be able to do?'

If alcoholics were weak willed individuals, wouldn't that flaw in their personality apply to all areas of their life? If there is really such a thing as an addictive personality then logic would dictate that the condition would apply to all areas and all alcoholics would also be obese, gambling addicted, heroin injecting, glue sniffers. You are alcoholic because of a long-term chemical imbalance exasperated by your body's tendency to process alcohol differently from those annoying people who can just enjoy a glass of red wine with their steak and think nothing of putting the bottle away for another day.

Alcoholism is often stated to be a disease just like cancer. This is not true; a disease implies there is nothing you can do about it and that you may have contracted it without any conscious input on your part. This creates the innocent victim mentality that drinkers then use as a perfectly valid excuse for them to continue drinking to excess. Once labeled as such, they begin a 'pity party' that can last a lifetime. They declare how terrible it is to suffer from such a debilitating condition. Shrugging their shoulders, cursing their bad luck as they wash away their perceived problems with a stiff drink.

You have lost a fight that you never had any chance of winning. It is not your fault but it absolutely is your responsibility.

Problem drinking is not a disease it is a negative behavioral loop that appears to be so complicated that it may feel as though it is unbreakable. Many people state that they drink to make their problems go away, but at the same time they are aware of all the extra problems their drinking is creating. All your beliefs about why you drink are likely to be a Catch 22 situation.

For example... You are worried about money and don't want to spend the evening thinking about all those bills and so out comes the booze. The alcohol (which is a mild anesthetic) merely time shifts your problems forward another 24 hours and then adds an additional problem of alcohol withdrawal into the mix. Remember, you started drinking to forget the bills but the booze habit is costing you thousands of dollars each year, and if you didn't spend so much feeding your alcohol addiction you would probably be able to pay all the bills you are worrying about in the first place.

The average person who stops drinking as a result of reading this book or joining my online club goes on to save over $4000 per year. While money isn't strictly speaking a good enough reason to stop on its own, it is a very pleasant by-product of quitting. If you were offered a no strings pay rise of that size, wouldn't you gladly accept it?

So if saving money is only the byproduct of the process you might be wondering what the primary reason is. We will come to that in due course and at this point in Alcohol Lied to Me I would like to offer you a word of warning; It's important to read this book in the order it is written and not be tempted to skip ahead to find the magic bullet cure. You will find no such thing; it is the slow deconstruction of the lies alcohol has repeatedly told you over the years, and a growing understanding of why booze affects you the way it does that allows you to see it for what it is. More importantly, to stop believing that alcohol is somehow benefiting you.

There are no real benefits to booze, only illusions of positives. Everyone who consumes alcohol has inadvertently placed himself or herself in the mousetrap, some are moments away from disaster, others are a lifetime away. Slowly the mechanism is loaded and primed, over time you become more and more at risk of letting alcohol seize control of your life. You are effectively playing a virtual version of Russian roulette, but with booze as the bullet in your loaded gun. Every time you drink you pull the trigger, and one day the chamber will not be empty. There is only one-way to play this game safely, and that is to remove the bullet - or putting it another way - don't drink.

This killer product escapes virtually all our current regulations and safeguards because it has been around long enough to set its own precedent. The fact that 'everyone drinks' and our parents, grandfparents and generations as far back as we can recall also drank alcohol, makes us incorrectly be<u>lie</u>ve we are protected by the assumed 'safety in numbers' principle. Actually that is not true, no drinker really believes that he or she is protected because of the social proof of the drug, they are just pleased to have another weapon in their arsenal to justify their behaviour around a substance that we all inherently know is dangerous and unhealthy.

There is no safety in numbers with alcohol, just because everyone you know drinks does not make it a safe product, reduce your chances of getting addicted or suffering harm in some way. Whether one person plays Russian roulette or a billion people play the odds remain the same for each person holding the gun. Every pull of the trigger is a separate unique incident and is completely independent of and uninfluenced by all the other triggers being pulled at that time. Just because the people who surround you all appear to be 'in control' of their drinking does not give you licence to assume you will be affected by alcohol in a similar way.

Many people pick up this book still hanging onto the hope that they will be able to reduce their drinking down to a sensible amount. I would love to tell you that glorious compromise is possible, perhaps I would sell more books if I pretended that it is. However, integrity is important to me and I can't tell you anything but the hard facts and truth about this drug.

Reducing the amount of poison you are consuming is as helpful to you as closing an open porthole on the Titanic. If I were to advise you to cut down there would be an implication that drinking perhaps provides some benefits if consumed in small amounts. It doesn't, the most common objection to this statement comes from the 'red wine is good for your heart' brigade. Credit where it is due this is correct to a certain degree; there are indeed a lot of healthy antioxidants in a glass of red wine. But no more so than you would find in a glass of non-alcoholic grape juice, or a hand full of pomegranate seeds. If it's your heart you are concerned about, find an alternative to wine. But if you really are using that argument to continue drinking, I suspect it really has nothing to do with your health.

If wine is so good for your heart, why don't doctors break out the Merlot when a patient is rushed into hospital suffering from a heart attack?

When most people realize drinking has changed from a 'nice to have' into a 'must have' they try to cut down. If you had a reckless and thrill seeking friend who you discovered was in the habit of loading a single bullet into a revolver and playing Russian Roulette for kicks a few times a week would you really advise him to cut down and only do it at the weekend or to stop completely? In 'Alcohol Lied to Me' I am going to demonstrate in undeniable detail to you as the intelligent and informed human being I know you are, exactly why alcohol is something that you do not need, does not serve you, has absolutely no benefits to it and creates nothing but negatives in your life. Once you understand that everything you currently believe is just smoke and mirrors generated by a myriad of social and psychological sources, I won't need to help you stop drinking, you simply won't want to.

We start this journey together by discovering exactly why people drink alcohol to excess. Some will claim booze has uplifting qualities (this is simply not true as it is actually a mind anesthetic). While others will say they need it to chill out and relax, and you will discover later why this is equally as illogical. At this moment all you need to know is that there is only one reason why people get hooked on alcohol... it's an addictive drug that causes a chemical imbalance in the brain.

There are no other reasons; you are not a victim of a disease or prone to an addictive personality. There is really no such thing as an addictive personality; it's just a convenient way of shifting the blame away from us to something external and apparently outside our control.

If somebody who juggles knives got accidentally stabbed by one of them, would you say it was not his fault because he has a personality that is susceptible to knife injuries? Or would you assume it was bound to happen one day?

If you take an addictive substance you will get addicted, it is an automatic and logical conclusion to your actions (it was bound to happen one day). It has nothing to do with a perceived fault in your genetic make up. Surely if such a broad condition as an addictive personality really existed then you would be addicted to everything? You would consume mountains of mashed potato, vats of honey, kilos of sugar and so on, apportioning all blame to your damn addictive personality disorder.

The closest excuse you have to your drinking not being your fault is a possible genetic blip in your DNA that makes you predisposed to being highly likely to develop a problem with alcohol. Breakthroughs in a field of medical science called epigenetic inheritance have revealed some startling findings.

Meeri Kim, writing for the Washington Post says:

A newborn mouse pup, seemingly innocent to the workings of the world, may actually harbor generations' worth of information passed down by its ancestors.

In the experiment, researchers taught male mice to fear the smell of cherry blossoms by associating the scent with mild foot shocks. Two weeks later, they bred with females. The resulting pups were raised to adulthood having never been exposed to the smell.

Yet when the critters caught a whiff of it for the first time, they suddenly became anxious and fearful. They were even born with more cherry-blossom-detecting neurons in their noses and more brain space devoted to cherry-blossom-smelling.

The memory transmission extended out another generation when these male mice bred, and similar results were found.

Neuroscientists at Emory University found that genetic markers, thought to be wiped clean before birth, were used to transmit a single traumatic experience across generations, leaving behind traces in the behavior and anatomy of future pups.

The study, published online Sunday in the journal Nature Neuroscience, adds to a growing pile of evidence suggesting that characteristics outside of the strict genetic code may also be acquired from our parents through epigenetic inheritance. Epigenetics studies how molecules act as DNA markers that influence how the genome is read. We pick up these epigenetic markers during our lives and in various locations on our body as we develop and interact with our environment.

Through a process dubbed "reprogramming," these epigenetic markers were thought to be erased in the earliest stages of development in mammals. But recent research — this study included — has shown that some of these markers may survive to the next generation.

In the past decade, the once-controversial field of epigenetics has blossomed. But proving epigenetic inheritance can be a daunting, needle-in-a-haystack undertaking. Researchers need to measure changes in offspring behavior and neuroanatomy, as well as tease out epigenetic markers within the father's sperm.

The DNA itself doesn't change, but how the sequence is read can vary wildly depending on which parts are accessible. Even though all the cells in our bodies share the same DNA, these markers can silence all the irrelevant genes so that a skin cell can be a skin cell, and not a brain cell or a liver cell.

Does this mean we as humans have also inherited generations of fears and experiences? Quite possibly, say scientists. Studies on humans suggest that children and grandchildren may have felt the epigenetic impact of such traumatic events such as famine, the Holocaust and the Sept. 11, 2001, terrorist attacks.

We are still scratching the surface of this new and interesting research but what this helps to explain is why children of alcoholics are much more likely to also develop a problem. Whether it is the genetic inheritance or the social conditioning is a point that will be debated for years. What this doesn't mean is you can carry on drinking while pointing an accusing finger at your parents.

If you discovered that skin cancer runs in your family would you go sit in the midday sun everyday and then blame your mom and dad when the bad news arrived one day?

The main reason your drinking has become a problem is down to a deficiency of important chemicals in your brain. Inside your frontal lobes there are millions of transmitters and receivers. These control every aspect of your life and determine how you feel about literally everything you experience on a day-to-day basis. When the sun goes down at the end of the day, the drop in available light causes your brain to stop producing adrenaline and start manufacturing a neuro-chemical called melatonin, this clever chemical calms your mind and allows sleep to occur. If you take a substance that interferes with this natural process, such as caffeine, then you will find it very difficult to get to sleep because of the chemical imbalance.

Staying with the sleep example for a moment, there are a few other reasons why the chemicals may not be present in the quantity that you need for a healthy regular sleep pattern. The brain makes melatonin from another chemical called serotonin. This is what makes us feel good about ourselves, it's a happy drug naturally created by our body to manifest feelings of contentment and joy. Serotonin can only be made from an amino acid called Tryptophan. If your diet is poor or specifically lacking in foods that are a source of Tryptophan then you will have a serotonin deficiency. As a direct result of that you will also have a melatonin deficiency. You would experience the outcome of this condition by complaining of 'having trouble sleeping' in the short term. If this imbalance stays in place for enough time you would then begin to label yourself as 'an insomniac'.

The other way you can have a chemical imbalance (again staying with the sleep analogy) is by being genetically predisposed to it. If you are born with Tryptophan transmitters and receivers that do not work as well as they should then you will need to consume significantly more of the amino acid in your diet than a 'normal' person to get the same result.

Incorrect brain chemistry makes you miserable!

Alcohol is a toxin that interferes with brain chemistry; unbalanced brain chemistry makes you unhappy, unsettled, stressed, and tired. All negative emotions that you believe can be fixed with a glass of the good stuff. This is a negative behavior loop like picking at a scab because it hurts. The more you pick at it the worst it gets, and yet you just can't leave it alone. You are stressed because alcohol has created a chemical imbalance in your brain, so you have a drink to unwind. The alcohol goes on to create more chemical imbalances to ensure you also feel uncomfortable again the next day, ensuring the consumption of the drug continues.

If you owned a multimillion-dollar racehorse, is it fair to say that you would treat it with respect, stable it in the very best yard and feed it only the best premium food you could buy? Is it also equally reasonable to assume if you owned this valuable racehorse you probably wouldn't put poison in its food? You own a body that is quite frankly awe-inspiring in its beauty, complexity and power, and yet you deliberately consume poison and claim you do it in the name of being social.

Thankfully, as a result of millions of years of evolution your body is pretty smart, it can sense when there is a dangerous foreign substance in the blood stream. When you ingest any toxin your body will start a series of automatic processes to eliminate it from your system (as many a late night cab driver has discovered). First the liver converts the alcohol into another chemical called acetaldehyde, which is less dangerous to the vital organs.

Alcohol dependent people have slowly trained and conditioned their liver to become far too efficient at processing alcohol. No sooner has the drink flowed into their liver than it is processed into acetaldehyde. This means we problem drinkers always have vast quantities of this chemical in our blood.

This causes two major problems; firstly it acts as an opiate, which as you know is highly addictive (we effectively have to deal with a continuous drug overdose). The double whammy is at such a high level these powerful chemicals have a secondary action of ripping through brain cells like napalm. It interferes with the thousands of receptors, prevents your body from absorbing minerals and vitamins and interferes with brain chemicals to such an extent that it takes months for the body to repair the damage (if you would just give it chance).

When alcohol hits your brain it triggers an artificial release of powerful chemicals that create a high. Every time you use alcohol to simulate this response; the receiver in your brain responsible for detecting the chemicals gets damaged a little bit more. Over time this is why you need more and more booze to create the same effect you used to get from one drink. This tolerance to alcohol is often seen as something to be proud of, especially in men. Being able to knock back ten pints of strong lager and not fall over has apparently become a clear sign of a real man. Remove the testosterone and in reality a tolerance is the first clear sign that alcohol has already caused significant damage.

Because of this severe chemical imbalance you are pre-disposed to having a problem with alcohol, using will-power to try and stop is always going to be like oil up a hill. Fighting brain chemicals with 'will-power' is pointless; if you have ever had a general anesthetic you will know that when they inject you with the chemical they asses its effectiveness by challenging you to count to ten. You confidently begin the count but somewhere around four or five the lights go out, even if you wanted to fight the drug you would lose. There is no power in 'will-power'!

This rule applies as much to naturally generated chemicals as it does to artificial ones. If your brain is full of adrenaline you can't go to sleep, it is impossible no matter how much 'will-power' you use. A specific chemical in your brain creates all strong emotions from grief to love. Estrogen makes women want to mother and care for the young; testosterone makes men want to fight and have sex with things. Dopamine creates a feeling of contentment and so on. If you injected someone with adrenaline just before going into a cinema, it would be unreasonable of you to call him weak willed because he wouldn't sit still and watch the movie with you.

'Will-power' is completely ineffective against brain chemicals and so to stop drinking for good you have to alter the way you think about booze, you have to not drink because you genuinely don't want to, and not because you are being hard on yourself. You must ensure that you never have to use 'will-power' again. To get to this point you need to be aware that alcohol slowly turns us all into liars, we are programmed from a very young age to see alcohol as a faultless, natural, mood enhancing, confidence inducing, 'good times for all' product. And not the foul tasting, health destroying slow poison that it really is.

Before we go any further I need to tell you that I am not a doctor. Neither am I a self-righteous saint who has never put a foot wrong on the path of life. I am not here to judge you or heap a load of shame upon you. I am here with you now because, in essence, I am the same as you. I too let alcohol control my life for over 17 years; the only difference between you and me now, is I am sitting outside the mousetrap looking at you sitting on it, like a greedy mouse that thinks he has discovered something amazing. Because I have been in the trap and experienced it, I know how you feel about giving up the drink. I know how many hundreds of times you have woken up ashamed of yourself, making veiled promises never to drink again. I know that you desperately want to give up this poison but I am also deeply aware that at the same time the thought of spending the rest of your life without drink appears at first thought to be a life not worth living.

The fact that you are reading this book means at some level you still believe that alcohol is a benefit to you. If you didn't believe that then you simply wouldn't drink and you wouldn't need me.

For most alcohol dependent people, a life without a drink appears empty and pointless. You may even be tempted to throw such arguments as:

- ☐ 'How can you go to a party and not drink?
- ☐ Am I destined to be the boring, party pooper for the rest of my life?'
- ☐ 'How can I go on holiday without drinking?'
- ☐ 'What am I going to do to relax/steady my nerve/get to sleep'... you can insert your own lie here if you want – but that's really all it is – a lie!

While you can't physically see any of the particles that make up the air that we breathe, you know that it is a mix of different gases, with oxygen being the most vital. You can't point to oxygen and prove it to me, but if I approached you today and told you that there is no oxygen in air, you wouldn't give any credence to my claim. Unless you are a physicist this probably isn't because of your irrefutable scientific knowledge or your ability to prove the existence of oxygen at the drop of a hat. It is purely because people you respect and trust have taught you this. You have been programmed to believe this from a very early age. The belief that we breathe oxygen is so engrained into the collective wisdom of society that it has become an undeniable fact.

Similarly, for thousands of years it was a statement of fact that the earth was flat. Repetition is the mother of learning, and so beliefs that have been repeated and observed many times over and by many different people become hard-wired facts in our collective intellect.

Alcohol and celebration are natural bed fellows right? All our perception of booze comes from society's collective opinion of it. Just as we were wrong about the earth being flat, we are collectively incorrect about what alcohol gives us. Some drinkers are so well programmed that at the mere suggestion from me that alcohol is not the nectar of the gods but rather a foul tasting, life destroying drug, they will instantly and aggressively disagree. If you find yourself saying 'well that's wrong for a start, I genuinely do like the taste of alcohol', I can promise you here and now you are at the point where your lies are so profound and so deeply ingrained in your subconscious that you can't even tell they are lies anymore.

With that depressing assessment established I want to give you two big reasons to be excited about where you are. Firstly, you not only bought the book but you opened it and started reading. This might sound like no big deal but let me tell you that over half the people who pick up a book to help address their drinking problem never even open it! Secondly, I am going to show you how to beat this drug in a completely easy and pain free way. Stay with me for the rest of this book and I will prove to you not only that alcohol is vile tasting, but also that deep down inside you instinctively know this already.

Once you start to see alcohol for what it really is then stopping becomes the byproduct of your new knowledge... you don't have to do anything – it just happens of its own accord.

Chapter Three
Where is the power?

In the 1980's when my friends' father had a new computer installed at his business premises, we all gathered in the street to watch its arrival. Such was its size the entire roof of the building had been removed to accommodate its installation. It arrived on the back of a flat bed truck and was hoisted into position with a crane that had also been hired at great expense to complete the delivery. An entire office had been cleared and made available for it, and yet it was capable of no more than the basic functions of our modern day calculators. In the realm of information technology we have progressed a long way in a short time, to the point where we now casually carry mobile phones with ten thousand times the computing power than that goliath of a machine.

You only need to look back at some of the predictions made for computers by the popular science magazines of the day to realize just how much we have exceeded expectations. The world wide market was predicted at one point to be just five machines, while another publication proudly declared that one day all computers would weigh less than 1.5 tonnes!

Today the machines our children use just to play computer games on have infinitely more processing and memory than the machines we used in the space technology that thrust the first man into outer space. However, while mankind can crow about its computerized revolution, despite these advances we have still only created a device with less than 1% of the power of the human mind. You can learn even the most complex of computer languages within five years, and yet you can spend a lifetime not quite getting to grips with the possibilities of your own internal computer.

Programmers spend years in training, diligently understanding the power of their machine before they start to generate code of any value. One of the first lessons they learn is through the acronym GIGO, which stands for Garbage In, Garbage Out. Sadly most people don't apply the same discipline to programming their own internal computer, a machine with the power to create literally anything.

Everything that you believe is wrong with your life exists purely because of bad programming in your subconscious mind. If you are overweight and unhappy about the size or shape of your body, it is due to a subconscious level belief that you actually want to be in that state. That's right I am saying if you are fat then it's probably because your subconscious believes that's what you want! Many will object in the strongest terms to a statement like that, but you can't possibly know at a conscious level what is stored in your subconscious mind. It would be akin to claiming you can carry the world's oceans in an eggcup. For the moment I would ask you to suspend your disbelief and stick with me as I explain.

This principle applies to everything that you would describe as good and or bad in your life.

A dependence on alcohol and other drugs is partly the unconscious belief that those chemicals are the best way to deal with pain being generated by your conscious thoughts. The perception that being seen in an expensive and flashy looking sports car makes you look more important to other people is a scenario generated by your egoic mind that has been repeated enough to become a subconscious belief. Perhaps from this point on it may be better to refer to beliefs like this as nothing more than a lie, the word believe even has the word lie in the middle of it as a reminder. The ego will attach itself to anything that hints at power, control or permanency. It is the part of you that is afraid of death and it will spend your entire lifetime in a blind panic about that one event. If it can demonstrate in anyway that you are more significant than other people or you are more in control then it will do just that.

When desires of the ego become so embedded in our image of ourselves they become automatic or subconscious, this is dangerous and self-destructive because of the immense power available to this part of you. The subconscious has a direct line to the divine power of the soul.

STOP! I feel an objection coming on, 'If the subconscious has the power of the soul, why doesn't it prevent the bad instructions from being completed, why on earth would it sit back and allow a self-destructive programme like alcoholism to run?' Firstly let me assure you I am not about to go 'all spiritual' on you just because I mentioned your soul. There is no religious element to this cure but let's deal in fact to fully understand how our brain operates. It is commonly accepted that our mind is split into two unequal halves that allow us to experience life on contrasting levels; consciously, with our thinking mind, and unconsciously, with the infinitely larger and more powerful part of our mind we call the subconscious.

Nothing portrays the delusion of power held by the conscious or egoic mind quite like the story of a little dog named Biba. Biba was the nasty little Jack Russell terrier my girlfriend had when I was 16 years old. This dog had a serious attitude problem; it was no bigger than a sofa cushion but had the aggression and belief that it was a fearsome Rottweiler. Every time I would visit my girlfriend, admittedly hoping for a bit of alone time with her, Biba would sit in the window watching me walk up the path to the house. Before I even had chance to knock on the door it would launch its pathetic and laughable attack, occasionally I would see a flash of its little white needle-like teeth through the letterbox.

Once inside it would sit on my girlfriends lap snarling at me. This one foot high, ten pound deluded animal actually looked at me, a 6'1", 14 stone man, and thought 'just let me at him and I will rip him to pieces'. The reality, as Biba often discovered, is that he was so small I could remove him from the room without even bending over. Simply by placing my shoe under his belly I could lift him and carry him out into the kitchen on the end of my foot, his legs kicking and teeth snapping all the way. With a grin across my face I would lock him in before sauntering back to my girlfriend, all the way listening to the furious muffled barking. For her sake I would agree with her that he was indeed a little cutie, I didn't believe that letting her know my true feelings for this repulsive little rat would have done me any favors.

Biba is how I see the conscious mind; it is a small, inefficient part of your mind that thinks it's much bigger and more important than it really is. It also has all the decorum and attitude of that little dog too. Your ego is the voice in your head that judges and questions everything in and around your life. As a child, as you stood on the starting line of the school race and the ego was there whispering in your ear. What is whispered is unique to you and what your ego wanted at that moment (some believed they could win – and they did, some believed they couldn't – and they lost).

The voice begins quiet and grows as strong as you will let it. Ever present in all areas of your life; at home, work and even socially. When you walk into a bar as a singleton it is the voice that tells you that you are more attractive and good looking than that person, but less so than another. As you watch a person drive past you in the automobile of your dreams it is the voice that tells you how you should feel about that person's public display of success. It either views the scene as something that you should also have (and need to be happy) or as an example of your lack of self worth. Of course both assessments are pointless and do not serve you but the ego is constantly looking for things to attach itself to. Books such as Rhonda Byrne's 'The Secret' try to make you aware of this instinctive reaction of the ego, and instead of responding as the ego dictates, instead it encourages you to make positive statements of intent instead. Suggesting instead of envy you see yourself sitting in that car and enjoy the positive image you have painted in your minds eye.

This is laudable and certainly better than any negative emotion, but again, if it is purely will-power arguing with the ego, it is largely pointless. It is for this reason that so many try the techniques described in 'The Secret' and other 'law of attraction' books and give up when they see little evidence of success. The real secret of manifestation is to understand that only the subconscious can create. And it does this in spite of the continuous diatribe coming from the ego. In short, you can say anything you want about yourself, it doesn't make the slightest bit of difference to what you get (unless you believe it). I can wake up every morning, stand in front of the bathroom mirror and with all the confidence and positive mental attitude I can muster, state that I am a professional football player. Unless I subconsciously believe that is even possible, then the chance of it becoming reality are somewhere between slim and none.

On one side of the coin this appears frustrating that we can't manifest our desires so easily, but on the other side and with some knowledge of the perfectly horrendous scenarios our thinking mind can create, it's probably for the best. Have you ever stood on top of a tall building and wondered just for the briefest of moments what it would feel like if you fell? With that in mind ask yourself do you still want to give the conscious mind the power to manifest the stuff of your imagination?

We all allow the ego to become so vocal that we begin to believe that it is who we are; we actually become the voice in our head. This is ultimately the source of all unhappiness and discontentment in life. The ultimate illusionist responsible for all the pain, but a master at laying the blame elsewhere, all input from this voice is generated by the need to avoid fear. With that in mind, it's not difficult to see why egoic dreams and indeed any desire born of a negative emotion, is unlikely to be beneficial in the long run. The conscious mind simply can't stop judging and answering questions, even if it doesn't know the answer. Such is the predictability of the ego that I can demonstrate its weakness with a few statements and questions that I would like you to try NOT to answer.

"What is 2+2"?
"What color are your eyes"?
"Whatever you do, don't think of an elephant"!

Like a puppy chasing a ball, your conscious cannot help itself; it simply must answer all questions asked of it. This isn't entirely a problem, as without this feature of the human mind, you would be dead by now. While you're conscious mind comes up with some pretty ill advised opinions about you and what you need to be happy, it also does a job of protecting you by judging all the situations in which you find yourself on a daily basis.

As you stand on the side of a busy road waiting to cross, your conscious mind evaluates the speed and distance of approaching traffic and decides at what point it is safe for you to cross the road. The reason why young people and the elderly are more at risk of injury in these situations is further evidence of the weakness of the ego. Children do not have enough information to accurately judge the risk, and the elderly are using outdated perceptions.

The conscious uses what it believes to be true to make the judgment. No doubt at some point when you were a child you picked up a hot pan on the stove and discovered quite quickly how much a burn can hurt. The lack of knowledge meant your conscious was incapable of judging the situation as a threat, but from that point on you will be much more cautious in the same environment. Taking this into consideration, you may now feel some gratitude towards your ego for acting so effectively at these points and saving you from serious harm. However, you should also be able to see that they are all motivated by nothing positive but rather the simple desire to avoid pain/fear. Everything the ego does comes from this starting point, and it is unwise to mistake its protection for care, the ego has no regard for your best interests, it only cares about what it wants. Sometimes the by-product of what the ego desires coincidently serves your 'well-being' at the same time, but it is not there by design, you just got lucky on that occasion.

The ego is quite willing to cause you immense suffering purely to get to the outcome it desires. Should the ego desire a specific material possession (or rather the feelings generated by attainment), it will apply massive pressure in the form of emotional pain until you give it what it wants. Then of course, as soon as you comply it rewards you briefly before beginning the process over again with even more intensity. This book is taking you on a journey of awareness and part of that is developing the ability to observe the ego as a third person trying to manipulate you rather than believe that you and your ego are one and the same.

If by this point you are not feeling too schizophrenic, let's talk about the larger and significantly more powerful subconscious. A polar opposite to the ego, the unconscious mind judges nothing; it is completely at peace and feels no need to compare you to others. It wants for nothing, needs nothing and fears nothing, operating in a divine state, existing purely in the moment. Nothing that has gone before is relevant, and the future is considered equally unimportant. The only thing that has relevance is the now, and in each and every moment your subconscious dutifully completes the programs that reside within itself with perfect accuracy. This is why you don't have to consciously beat your heart, control your body temperature or any of the other millions of functions happening in your body every second of every day.

During the time it has taken for you to read that last sentence, your subconscious has destroyed and replaced

50,000,000 cells in your body, its power is simply awe-inspiring. Ridiculously, sitting at the feet of the awesome power and like Biba, the bad attitude dog, your conscious mind actually believes it is equal to, if not more powerful. This is the very embodiment of arrogance and pomposity; it's like a three legged, blind donkey insisting it could take on and beat a multimillion-dollar racehorse. The truth is like a bully challenged to really show what he is made of. If your ego suddenly became responsible for everything currently looked after by the subconscious, you would be dead in less than a second.

Why do most people in the western world drink?

Because the conscious mind contains the ego and the ego is insane! It creates all the misery and then comes up with completely ineffective ways to deal with the problems. It lives in a constant state of pure terror, always trying to manipulate you to make that fear dissipate. Like a whirling dervish in a fine china store the ego stumbles through life predicting doom and gloom. It creates chaos and then points the finger of blame at someone else, anyone else. As you respond to this drama and try your best to avoid the tidal wave of destruction the ego would create given the chance, you express these sensations as evidence of life being difficult, hard and a constant struggle.

Spiritual souls such as monks and Buddhist teachers know that resisting the demands of ego and being at peace with whatever happens in this lifetime is the secret to true happiness. They know at a deep and profound level that life is not the beginning or the end but rather a continuation and so the ego loses its leverage over them. When their ego screams and shouts about whatever material possession it has decided they should have to be truly happy, these enlightened folk ignore it and simply stay quietly in the moment. This does not mean their life is easy or that they don't suffer but they do choose to accept responsibility for all of life's challenges rather than seek to blame and struggle to retake control.

Sadly the vast majority of us are not able to be recognize the ego because we have become too interlinked with it.

The judgments and demands in our head, we believe to be our own and we respond accordingly. Thrashing about trying to control the uncontrollable and it inevitably makes us miserable and stressed. Alcohol sedates the conscious mind by acting as a brief distraction. All addictions serve the same purpose; whether it is over eating, drugs or the modern and trendy conditions, such as Hollywood's new favorite, 'sex addiction'. It's a bit like when you pretend to throw a ball for a dog. For a few seconds the dog runs off in the direction you pretended to throw, it stops and looks around for the ball before realizing it was a trick and then it comes pouncing back to you.

You are using a chemical distraction for the ego! So why alcohol for you and not something else, you might ask? That is a question with a million answers, but you can be sure it's no accident. Genetics and your environment undoubtedly play a part, but these all cause the same problem; a chemical imbalance in the brain. If you can prevent the imbalance and change your belief structure around alcohol, you will be cured.

I am not denying that DNA plays a part; you are indeed significantly more likely to have a drink problem if your parents were dependent upon alcohol. This could be down to you picking up equally ineffective transmitters and receivers as your parents had, or purely down to a psychological trait called social proof, i.e. the tendency to accept as true what you witness repeatedly by those around you.

If you grew up watching your father come home from work and before he even got his hat and coat off, a large Whiskey was gripped firmly in his hand, it's not difficult to see why you would develop the belief that this is normal behavior. If your father (whom you respect and admire) uses alcohol and appears to enjoy it so much, then it must be a benefit that you are currently being deprived of. Your ego will not accept that situation, and as soon as it can it will correct that injustice. This is why at the age of 12 you find yourself sneaking a sip of your dad's whiskey and wondering why it tastes so awful.

It is also equally likely that you have inherited the same over-efficient liver and infective receptors in the brain that most alcoholics are victim to. When most people take a drink of alcohol it causes the hypothalamus in the brain to release a powerful neurotransmitter called Dopamine. For most people, 'those goody two shoes types' who appear to be able to have a glass of Champagne at a party without desperately looking for the next one, the Dopamine release is tiny. It creates a small sense of well-being but there is not enough chemical excreted and quickly enough to be addictive (in your sense of the word).

To give you a non-booze related comparison, imagine if some people were similarly desensitized to sweet and sugary food like chocolate or cake, as you are to alcohol. Imagine, for these people with a 'cake tolerance' to get the same taste and enjoyment that you get from a single piece of chocolate cake they would have to eat 30 slices (just to get the slightest hint of the kick you get), do you think any of them would get addicted? It's very hard to get hooked on something that requires that level of interaction. This is why alcoholism carries such a stigma, for most people it seems like completely nonsensical behavior. In exactly the same way that you would frown at, and chastise someone who shoveled down 30 pieces of cake in a sitting.

In the problem drinker, more often than not the dopamine released as a response to detection of alcohol in the blood stream is massive. Suddenly the body is awash with huge quantities of a powerful and addictive drug. So much so that the sheer onslaught of chemicals damages the receivers in the brain in the same way that continuous loud noise causes damage to hearing. People who have worked with noisy machinery all their lives have a diminished ability to receive sound at the correct level and need to be fitted with a hearing aid to amplify the volume. Drinkers have a diminished ability to receive neuro-transmitters and need higher quantities of the drug to recreate the original high.

The chemical receptors in the alcohol dependents' brain are so numbed from the 'noise' of the continual abuse that they simple cannot detect the feel good chemicals produced by the body at natural levels. Only when a drug creates the massive flood of the chemicals are they able to feel 'normal'. The good news is, if you stop drinking, within a few weeks you will start to feel better, and within six months to a year your receptors will be repaired.

The easy option here is to declare that your drinking is not your fault; you are cursed with a defective hypothalamus. Nice try, but this only explains why you choose to be dependent on alcohol rather than another addiction. In other words, if it wasn't the booze, it would be something else. The problem lies not with the alcohol, but with your ego or conscious mind believing it is in control of your life. The ego has selected alcohol to address an underlying problem, and this is why I say you are not an alcoholic. Your use of booze is a symptom of a problem, not the actual problem itself.

All worry, anxiety, stress and depression come directly from the conscious minds delusion that it can predict the future. That little voice inside your head that comes up with a thousand things that could go wrong is simply the ego trying to punch above its weight. The ego is also the hidden voice that judges you and deems you unworthy of some things based on experiences of the past. Girls who grew up with an abusive and controlling father often go on to marry abusive and controlling husbands. This is a pure manifestation of the ego using the past to try and predict the future.

The ego, unable to accept its own lack of power, tries in vain to control the uncontrollable. Every moment of life is experienced in the present, right here in this moment neither the past nor the future exists. Those enlightened souls who live their lives in the moment NEVER, and I really do mean NEVER, have addictions.

Having no concern for the past and not knowing what the future might bring, to the egoic mind is pure chaos and it simply can't accept it. You will no doubt have heard of the human drive to apply order to chaos, well this comes directly from the conscious mind trying to predict the next series of events using the past as a reverse projector (assuming what went wrong before will happen again).

Does this sound crazy or schizophrenic?

Good, because it is! The ego is insane and its continuous dissatisfaction with life and its never ending lists of needs, desires and fears causes the running dialogue in your mind that makes you crave alcohol as a panacea. Drinking hits the pause button on this monologue, and for a brief moment the pain stops, the dopamine sedates the ego and you take a small step towards peace. The futility of using any addiction to pause the tape so to speak, is that when the fix wears off the tape begins to play again, you haven't missed any of the gloomy recording. At no point did you fast forward, you still have all the pain to go through from the moment you hit pause. Plus, you now have the additional problem of withdrawal from an addictive drug and the chemical imbalance that comes from that.

By now you should be able to see why 'will-power' has been so ineffectual in the past. One of the biggest problems with 'will-power' is the associated feeling that you are a bad person or doing something wrong. Then ultimately when you fail to force the bad habit into abeyance you are left with the demoralizing sensation of failure and hopelessness. Let's get this straight, just because you are struggling with alcohol addiction does not mean you are a bad person or a failure. Think of it like this...

Sleeping tablets make you fall asleep, anti-emetic tablets stop you being sick and addictive drugs get you addicted. It would not be your fault if you fell asleep after taking a sleeping tablet and therefore we must apply the same blame to alcohol and not to you.

Alcoholism is a symptom of the problem and not the problem itself! The complexities of why we get addicted to anything are hugely misunderstood. The route out of this destructive cycle has nothing to do with drinking, what you will learn as we progress through this book, is that the cure for your problem lies here in this moment, and is not some future destination you will arrive at one day.

Chapter Four
"You are not alone"

So, more than 80% of the adult population of the western world drink alcohol, more than 80% of those have a problem, and 80% of them will never admit it. The first thing you should be proud of is that you have taken a step that most people will never have the courage to take; you have admitted that you are worried. Not only that, you have paid your hard earned money and put your trust in my system to help you regain control of your drinking. I can't express this strongly enough; this small act puts you in the top 20% of people. Admitting you have a problem effectively means you are already 50% of the way down the road to full recovery.

STOP: Before you break open the champagne (or whatever your chosen brand of attractively packaged poison is), let me give you a word of warning: Despite what you have been told in the past, 'knowledge is not power', but rather 'knowledge is only potential power!' If you do nothing with it, it's useless data. The shocking fact is that 20% of the people who buy a self help book, DVD or course such as this one will never listen to a word, put the DVD in the player or even open the book to the first page. It's as though the act of buying the book was good enough 'for now'. It's a similar act of procrastination of all those people who proudly announce 'the diet starts Monday!' Surely, if they were really committed to losing the weight they would start the diet immediately, without delay! Yet, the diet always starts Monday because it's a free license to eat like a pig all weekend while lying to yourself that you have all the good intentions in the world to repair the damage on Monday.

By the way... the reason diets don't work for 95% of people who use them is; Diets also rely on 'will-power' and so they make you unhappy and fat, which is exactly why they have hidden a secret warning in the first three letters of the word diet.

Now you have started on this monumental journey, do not stop. Neither should you skip forward to try and find the secret or quick fix to your problem. You did not go to bed one night in control of alcohol and wake up the next morning an 'alcoholic'. This drug has taken years, sometimes even decades to alter physical pathways in your brain, there is no quick fix – but that doesn't mean it has to be painful, or that you need to suffer. The old adage of 'No Pain – No Gain' does not apply here and trying to fight your way out of this situation is actually why you have failed to cut down in the past. It's going to take some effort on your behalf, and you may mess up every now and again, but you know what... it's not a big deal. You are not a robot and as long as you keep working with me for the next 21 days you are going to come out of this process stronger, cleaner and happier than you have been in a long, long time.

Unless of course you are STILL asking the question 'do I have a problem with drinking?' That really is the question I get asked more than any other, if I had a penny for every email I have had from people describing their habits and then asking 'do you think I have a problem?' I would be well on my way to a very happy retirement.

Let me answer that question for you now by first translating the question into what I believe you are REALLY asking: 'I like drinking, but I am worried I can't stop, can you tell me I don't have a problem and make the worry go away so I can carry on?'

You have an unnatural relationship with alcohol, and that is why you are here. Normal 'social' poison drinkers don't ever think about their drinking habits, never mind search the Internet for help and advice, or go as far as to purchase a book like this. If you have to question your behavior around alcohol, it's the clearest sign you can get that alcohol has become a fixation. Try not to beat yourself up about this because in reality, it's not actually possible for anyone to have an natural relationship with alcohol because it is a toxin packaged in pretty bottles. The belief that anyone can be a 'normal/social' drinker of a poison is a myth, how can it be possible to be a normal user of an addictive drug?

If a friend confided in you that he was a glue sniffer, but as kept his solvent abuse strictly limited to weekends, would you declare him a social glue sniffer? Replace glue with heroin... would your friend be a 'normal' heroin user? You may think I am going to extremes to prove a point here, but there are only two differences between alcohol and heroin, and the first is social acceptability. Alcohol is socially acceptable and heroin is not. From birth we are exposed to booze being portrayed in a positive light, a substance that we are happy to ignore the logic of, and assume that it has some sort of smart technology behind it.

Somehow we believe alcohol has the ability to make us more aware of positive emotions and feelings, and also claim it can also dampen down negative emotions and help us forget our problems. Only a substance that could change its chemical make-up could possibly achieve this. There is nothing intelligent about alcohol, remember, it is the waste product of decaying vegetable matter, not a lab designed smart drug.

The second difference between alcohol and other class A street drugs is all about timescale. It is very easy to become addicted to heroin in a short space of time because the kick (withdrawal) is condensed into a smaller time instead of the slow build up of discomfort that you get from alcohol withdrawal; heroin users get massive and unbearable amounts of pain in a relatively short space of time. That is where the differences end, they both can and will try to kill you. They will both do significant permanent damage to your health, relationships, finances, and state of mind, and they will both twist your perception dramatically enough to make you believe that while they are doing all this negative stuff, they are also in some way a benefit to you at the same time.

I believe that alcohol is infinitely more deceptive than heroin because of the long and drawn out way it drags the user into a trap. Alcohol dependency can takes decades to reach its peak addiction. It creeps up on you so slowly that for the longest time you have no idea your drinking has become unusual. You are encouraged to look the other way and ignore the slight of hand happening in your peripheral vision by societies love affair with this drug.

This is illogical, and at your core (subconscious) you understand this. The single strongest human need is that of self-preservation, you have no control over this. Your core programme is to stay alive at all costs; it's hard wired into every cell in your body. And every one of those cells knows that alcohol is extremely dangerous to you. The body constantly tries to warn you, but you have learned to see those warning signs as positives rather than negatives.

• We may go red in the face or start to sweat, and we lie to ourselves and see it as a sign of merriment.

• We lose our inhibitions (which are there to protect us) and we lie to ourselves that the booze has boosted our confidence and self esteem.

• We drink so much that the brain loses control of our ability to talk, our speech becomes slurred and yet we still don't see it as a warning that something is wrong.

• Our brains are misfiring so frequently and unpredictable that we can't walk straight, and yet we joke about it.

• Eventually we get to the point where our body says enough is enough, it pushes the emergency button, which says I must get this poison out of the system, and it forces you to throw up. Do we listen at this point? No. We lie to ourselves that it's the sign of a good night.

• Maybe the hangover should be a sign of the damage we did, but no. We have been told over and over again since we were small that a hangover is natural. It's just what happens when you drink. Think about it if you got the same feelings the day after you ate a piece of toast, would you even consider eating toast again?

Perhaps you are here reading these words under duress; maybe a concerned family member, friend or employer bought this book for you. I can't tell you how many concerned partners I've met who are in relationships with people who resolutely insist they don't have a problem with drink. I am yet to meet a single one of these individuals that proves their partner wrong.

Part of 'Alcohol Lied to Me' is all about helping you understand how you got to where you are today, and why we are all tricked and deceived by alcohol. How this poison is packaged up into attractive looking bottles and marketed around the world with multibillion-dollar advertising campaigns. Booze is the ultimate wolf in sheep's clothing, known to liver consultants and medical professionals around the world (who diligently mop up our mess) as the silent killer. Often before you even know there is a problem, the damage done.

Chapter Five
"Alcohol – our favorite drug"

The great relay race of drinking nearly always starts with your parents, and indeed their parents before them, and so on. When you are born into this world, you enter as a completely helpless, weak and fragile individual driven by the need for love. Strange looking giants surround you and over a space of time you notice that two of these giants appear to have taken an interest in you. They feed you, care for you and love you (despite your crying and constant demands on their time).

For many years, these two people are given the accreditation of being Gods in your eyes. It is completely inconceivable that they could ever be wrong or would ever lie or mislead you. Their words and actions are your gospel, and before the age of 5 you blindly accept information from this source without question. Everything you learn and witness at this tender age is stored permanently in your subconscious as a pure fact.

In short, what you teach, show and expose your children to before the age of 5 will have a significant impact on how they turn out as adults.

Your experience with alcohol started from the moment you entered the world, it's more than likely the giants around you even used this poison to celebrate your arrival into the world. As you watched the giants popping corks out of attractive looking bottles, great smiles grew across their faces and laughter filled the room; what an amazing liquid this must be.

How strange that such a beautiful and unique gift is given to two happy people and they choose to herald the joyous arrival with a nice glass of a foul tasting depressant that removes our ability to consciously experience the wonderful things going on around us.

Alcohol is a tradition that has been passed down the family line from generation to generation (like a defective gene or biological bad penny). You only need to change the drug to see the truth behind the lies. If a bunch of friends came around to your house to meet your new baby and they all insisted on taking cocaine to wet the baby's head, I am sure you would have something to say.

I can make this point even clearer if you take a drug that has only recently become unacceptable. It's not so long back that a fine cigar was mandatory for the men folk to welcome in a new addition to the family. These days smoking over a newborn child would be seen as the height of irresponsibility.

The story of the humble cigarette is interesting to make a comparison with. Many of my heavy drinking friends would never dream of smoking, they believe it to be an anti social habit and exceptionally bad for you. Across Europe these days every packet of cigarette comes emblazoned with horrific images of diseased lungs and the cancer infested bodies of smokers. But you really don't have to go too far back in time and this collective disgust for smoking was certainly not the norm. I grew up in England in the seventies, a time when smoking was commonplace. Restaurants, theatres and in fact all public places were permanently shrouded in a thick fog of cigarette smoke. Candy stores even sold fake sugar based cigarettes and cigars so children could pretend to smoke, just like their older family members. Can you imagine the public outrage today if I confectionary company tried to promote their 'training cigarettes' for children?

At the time this was normal and unquestioned by even the most well intentioned and intelligent of people. Go back a little further and it seems incredible that doctors once suggested smoking as a cure for various aliments. For a long time cigarettes were even marketed as a health enhancing product. It took decades for that opinion to change and even now the job is still less only half done.

Still the overriding opinion of western society is that smoking is much worse for you than drinking alcohol. However, according to the World Health Organization's own chart of what is most likely to kill us; tobacco use ranks sixth. What surprises most people is alcohol on that very same chart comes in a third, wiping out over

2,500,000 people every year. Not bad going for a harmless social pleasantry!

Let's return to the thought of smoking over a newborn baby in this day and age. I know there will be some objections that it is not a fair comparison. You may object and claim that smoking over a newborn is only bad because of the passive smoke you are enforcing the baby to inhale. As it is not possible to passively drink, it cannot be fairly compared to drinking. This is correct in physical terms but remember, everything you see at this impressionable age is received as a pure fact. From the child's point of view, why would one of the loving giants do something that is dangerous or wrong? Essentially, if their God drinks and it makes them happy, it must be something wonderful. Over the space of a few years the child will witness many thousands of occasions where pleasure is linked to alcohol. Birthday parties, Christmas, Mothers Day, Valentines Day and even family BBQ's. Repetition is the mother of all learning.

It's the same reason why it's unthinkable to consider throwing a party without having alcoholic drinks. You do it because it's always been done, but if your parents had not passed the poison chalice onto you, and you don't pass it onto your children, the tradition becomes diluted and eventually ineffectual. We don't have to conduct an extravagant experiment over several generations to prove this point. You only need to look at other cultures; Hinduism has many festivals and celebrations that are full of merriment, singing and dancing without a single drop of alcohol passing anyone's lips.

Alcohol does not make a party – people do! But just try throwing a party in your part of the world without any alcohol and half your guests will leave and go to the nearest pub. It's not that drinking creates fun, it's more that people who are out of control of their drinking are miserable without alcohol and can't think about anything else when they are without it. This isn't the fault of your party, it's the fault of society that teaches everyone of us how to get addicted to a powerful and deceptive drug, and then compounds the problem by making us believe that it's normal.

Most people who drink wine everyday claim they honestly like the taste of it. This is nonsense; alcohol tastes so bad that the drinks manufacturers essentially have to find increasingly potent ways to cover it up. The body is an amazing and sophisticated piece of natural engineering. Despite what lies you have taught yourself on a superficial level, you still cannot break the rules your body has created over millions of years of evolution. Right at the top of our hierarchy of needs is the need to protect life, to stay alive at all costs. This is hardwired into every cell, every molecule and every tiny atom of your being. You can't decide to stop your heart beating or never to breathe again. You can't because it breaks the ultimate built-in rule; that of ensuring self-preservation at all costs.

The reason pure alcohol tastes bad is the same reason rotting meat or moldy, fungus infested bread tastes bad.

Your body is warning you that you are consuming something that is putting you at risk. Think about it, in a hospital operating theatre, the room and the entire medical team that works in it must be 100% free of germs, bacteria and viral contaminants. So what do they scrub their hands with; not soap but alcohol. Because instantly on contact with any living organisms, it kills them dead! It pulls every bit of moisture out of their cells and causes them to implode in on themselves. At a micro cellular level, alcohol is a kin to thermo nuclear war; nothing survives. Do you honestly believe you have some amazing internal system to get around this fact? Somehow, when you consume this dangerous disinfectant it doesn't do the same level of damage because you have hidden it in a bit of cranberry juice.

Alcohol tastes horrible, you already know this but have forgotten, or as is more accurate, you have conditioned yourself to believe the opposite. As a hypnotherapist I can tell you that this is entirely possible and can be easily replicated in a relatively short space of time to prove the point. In hypnosis the conscious (thinking and judging) mind is bypassed, which means I can speak directly to the subconscious and implant beliefs without interference from the ego. Obviously, in therapy (and what you will find on the hypnosis tracks that accompany this book – available in the members area) all suggestions are positive and delivered for your benefit, but it is entirely possible for me to condition you to enjoy something deeply unpleasant, such as a hard punch on the arm! If while under hypnosis I hit you hard but told you it felt amazing and repeated that process many times and over several sessions, you would eventually begin to crave the experience.

You can see this feature of the human mind demonstrated in the most horrendous situations. When people are held captive by a sole individual and despite the fact that this person has abducted them, tortured and abused them, the victim slowly over time begins to develop feelings for the perpetrator. Despite suffering at the hands of this person, they become conditioned to their environment and begin to want to please the person who holds them against their will. This phenomenon has been studied at length by eminent psychologists and is known as 'Stockholm syndrome'.

To a certain degree I believe you are suffering from a form of this syndrome, alcohol has abused you for so long that you now firmly believe there is a benefit to you. You have fallen in love with a killer!

I say again, Alcohol tastes bad, your first interaction with it proved that point. When you first sneaked a drink of your father's neat whiskey, did it taste amazing? Or did it taste vile? Most people will say it tasted disgusting and they couldn't ever imagine getting hooked on something that tasted that bad. The taste of alcohol has not changed, so the only explanation for your current belief that it tastes good, is that you have changed. You have conditioned yourself to believe booze tastes good. Don't feel bad; you have had a significant helping hand from society and the advertising industry.

What you must understand from this point on is that what you previously believed about booze was a lie and nothing more. If I poured a glass of pure alcohol and asked you to dip your little finger in and taste it, I am sure you will agree it would taste horrible, indeed, if you drank that glass of liquid you would shortly be dead. Funny really because since birth you have been programmed to ignore this and instead believe that alcohol is natural and an everyday part of life that you must consume if you are to be considered by your peers as a fun and social member of the gang. This is a throw back to our primitive evolution, we are still pack animals to a certain extent, and this is another reason for our global addiction to this drug.

The second reason is best explained by a smarter man than I, a famous psychologist called Abraham Maslow. Maslow is known for establishing the theory of a hierarchy of needs, writing that human beings are motivated by unsatisfied needs, and that certain lower needs need to be satisfied before higher needs can be.

Although there is a continuous cycle of human wars, murder, and deceit, he believed that violence is not what human nature is meant to be like. Violence and other evils occur when human needs are thwarted. In other words, people who are deprived of lower needs, such as safety, may defend themselves by violent means. He did not believe that humans are violent because they enjoy violence. Or that they lie, cheat, and steal because they enjoy doing it.

According to Maslow, there are general types of needs (physiological, safety, love, and esteem) and they must be satisfied before a person can act unselfishly. He called these needs "deficiency needs". As long as we are motivated to satisfy these cravings, we are moving towards growth, toward self-actualization.

Satisfying needs is healthy, and blocking gratification makes us sick and unhappy. In other words, we are all "needs junkies" with cravings that must be satisfied and should be satisfied. If we don't concentrate on doing this we will literally become sick. 'Will-power' is an illusionary weapon created by the egoic mind. It's like your enemy giving you a plastic sword and saying 'here, use this to protect yourself if I ever attack you!' This is exactly why people have such a hard time trying to go cold turkey with their drinking. One morning you wake up and say, that's it I am never drinking again. By lunchtime you have a psychological itch so intense you are almost screaming inside.

Will-power does not work because it forces your subconscious and conscious mind into civil war. The exact same reason why the moment you go on a diet you become hungrier than you thought possible.

Here is the secret to stopping drinking; you need to attach more pleasure to not drinking than there is to drinking. You have to remove the need by understanding the truth about booze. It is not a social pleasantry but rather an attractively packaged poison. A multi billion dollar marketing campaign for the alcoholic drinks industry is working exceptionally hard to convince you otherwise, but you have to trust your gut on this one.

Let me put the point another way. I have two wonderful children who I love and adore more than life itself. Maybe you also have children yourself and you can understand my love and need to protect my children from the harms of the world? Let me ask you a question: If you had some strong rat poison for dealing with a tricky vermin infestation, would you keep it in a chocolate box and put it within reach of your kids?

Alcohol is similar to an anti-personnel landmine. You step on it and beyond a small clunk all appears fine... until you try and step off it. Then and only then you discover what a mess you are really in.

Our desire to drink is what we call a proponent need; this is a 'need' that has a powerful influence over our actions. Everyone has proponent needs, but those 'needs' will vary among individuals. A teenager may have a need to feel that he/she is accepted by a group. A heroin addict will need to satisfy his/her cravings for heroin to function normally in society, and because of the strength of the need they are unlikely to worry about acceptance by other people.

There is no difference between alcohol and heroin, or alcohol and nicotine. The only difference is alcohol is socially acceptable. But ask yourself this, if it had not yet been invented and I brought it to market tomorrow, do you think I would get it even half way through the rigorous testing process modern day food and beverages have to go through?

Around the world there is a very popular television programme called 'Dragon's Den', where would-be entrepreneurs pitch their ideas to already successful venture capitalists seeking investment. Can you imagine taking your fabulous new drink additive called alcohol before the Dragons and asking them to invest?

Entrepreneur: "Hello Dragons... I am here to ask for $1,000,000,000 to launch my new drink supplement called alcohol. Would you like to try a glass?"

A small sample of the product is poured into shot glasses for each of the investors in turn; cautiously they take a sip...

Dragons: "My God that tastes disgusting!"

Entrepreneur: "Yes, it does initially, but we have tested it quite extensively and find that people do eventually become accustomed to the taste. Plus, we use sweet tasting carrier beverages such as orange juice and cola to cover up the real taste. When they get used to it the consumer will feel amazing! Parties will go with a bang, everything seems funnier, and there is a massive euphoric sense of well being".

Dragons: "Sounds interesting, are there any down sides to this new drink?"

Entrepreneur: "Erm, well there is a slight risk of vomiting, sexually transmitted disease from unprotected sex, not to mention the violence and serious damage to careers, reputations and relationships. You probably need to be aware that several millions of our potential customers will have to die in agony from organ failure. Apart from that, I think this product has great potential".

Dragons: "I am not investing in that, I am out!"

Am I going to ridiculous extremes to make my point here? Perhaps. But no more ridiculous than people around the western world claiming that the disgusting liquid they took a sneaky drink of when their parents weren't looking as a kid, has somehow turned into a exquisite and delicious beverage. The booze tastes just as vile as it ever did, but you have allowed this attractively packaged poison to fit you with some very impressed rose-tinted glasses!

Here's an experiment for you, wait until Friday evening and go check your friends out of Facebook. You will see status after status along these lines:

"Wine O-Clock... I think so"
"Friday night and I can hear the beer monster calling'

"Friday night take away and a bottle of wine... it would be rude not to"

"Thank God it's the weekend, chilling out with a nice bottle of red"

"Enjoying a very large glass of wine... I love the weekends"

"Cheeky glass of wine on the go"

That last one particularly amuses me, that we could explain away what we are doing by adding a cute descriptive term before admitting the truth. You wouldn't hear this with any other drug would you? Imagine if we talked about heroin in the same way.

"Friday night, cheeky hit of heroin... it would be rude not to"

It's time to grow up and realize you have been scammed. Yes, you. The bright and worldly-wise individual who has a good job and a successful career. The very same person who achieved all that, has been fooled by the oldest trick in the book.

You have become addicted to a drug, and this has created a recurring psychological itch that makes you want to scratch it at regular intervals. You have created a deficiency need, and according to Abraham Maslow, when the deficiency needs are met: Instantly other and higher needs emerge, and these, rather than physiological hungers, dominate the person. And when these in turn are satisfied, again new (and still higher) needs emerge, and so on. As one desire is satisfied, another pops up to take its place. It is this automatic behavior pattern that means we never really get the motivation to focus on what needs we are serving. The ego once again complicates the matter by insisting on more. More gratification, more consumption, more love, more power just more!

We are complicated beings and our addiction to alcohol is just one cog in an intricate and needy machine. We are also addicted to love and significance. Which distracts our attention from the addiction we could actually do something about! Humans have a desire to belong to groups: clubs, work groups, religious groups, family, gangs, etc. We need to feel loved by others, not so much in a sexual way; I suppose another way of putting it would be to say that we need to feel significant. We need to be accepted by others. Performers appreciate applause. We need to be needed. Beer commercials, in addition to playing on sex, also often show how beer makes for camaraderie. When was the last time you saw a beer commercial with someone drinking beer alone?

But does alcohol really answer the social need within us; we like to get together and consume this drug but does it really create a sensation of love?

Ask yourself how you would feel about ordering a drink of alcohol in a room full of teetotalers. Perhaps group drinking creates a sensation of safety in numbers, it makes us feel like what we are doing is perfectly acceptable in the eyes of our peers. Plus we also get to witness people who are 'far more drunk' than us!

Alcohol is touted as the social drug but in actual fact it turns us into very anti-social individuals. We come loud and opinionated; in some cases it makes us aggressive and violent. Even the 'happy drunks' slur and talk nothing but pure gibberish as they fall over even the most obvious obstacle. Uncontrolled laughter, loss of bladder control, vomiting in the streets and in the back of taxi cabs are just a few of the accepted norms of this most social of drugs.

When you stop drinking you will look at all this universally endorsed chaos and see it for what it really is – group insanity on a global level.

Chapter Six
Lie down with dogs – get up with fleas

Another reason why quitting drinking using will-power is so difficult is that the social deck of cards is not stacked in your favor. Every part of aspirational western life is geared towards alcohol being a part of your overall success. If you become fabulously wealthy, one of the things you simply must have in your mansion in the country is a well-stocked cellar full of the finest wines from around the world.

Recently in the UK, a group of bankers were highly publicized for spending £40,000 on fine wine over the course of a single meal. The marketing machine behind alcohol is so much more devious and calculating than the one behind cigarettes ever was. Not only would they have you believe that wine is good for you, but they also suggest you are nobody unless you own the very best versions of their poison.

Let's take a look at Champagne, essentially fizzy white wine grown in an ever-expanding region of France. It ranges in price from $20 per bottle to many thousands of dollars a bottle. Even this overpriced, attractively packed plonk has its own inner circle of snobbery. I have been to media party's where guests have turned their nose up at a $30 bottle of Champagne and demanded better quality Crystal or Krug, costing upwards of $450 a bottle. These people are not more refined, a higher class or more educated, they are just more examples of individuals who have fallen for the biggest scam going but are using snobbery to cover it up.

In my book 'The Hypnotic Salesman' I talk about the two most powerful motivational forces in the world. They are the law of scarcity and the law of social proof. Scarcity is the most potent form of leverage there is. It is the reason why we will pay vast sums of money for rare diamonds and one off pieces of fine art. Objects that are in limited supply are attractive to our ego, owning these things give us a sense of being important and make us feel special.

The second major influencing force is the law of social proof. In 1968, the social psychologists Stanley Milgram, Leonard Bickman, and Lawrence Berkowitz decided to cause a little trouble. First they put a single person on a street corner and had him look up at an empty sky for sixty seconds. A tiny fraction of the passing pedestrians stopped to see what the guy was looking at, but most just walked past. Next time around, the psychologists put five skyward-looking men on the corner. This time, four times as many people stopped to gaze at the empty sky. When the psychologists put fifteen men on the corner, 45 percent of all passers by stopped, and increasing the cohort of observers yet again made more than 80 per cent of pedestrians tilt their heads and look up.

This study appears at first glance, to be another demonstration of people's willingness to conform. But in fact it illustrated something different, namely the idea of "social proof", which is the tendency to assume that if lots of people are doing something or believe something, there must be a good reason why. This is different from conformity: people are not looking up at the sky because of peer pressure or a fear of being reprimanded. They're looking up at the sky because they assume - quite reasonably - that lots of people wouldn't be gazing upward if there weren't something to see. That's why the crowd becomes more influential as it becomes bigger: every additional person is proof that something important is happening. And the governing assumption seems to be that when things are uncertain, the best thing to do is just to follow along.

Social proof used to back up smoking as an acceptable habit, literally everyone was doing it and therefore the unspoken opinion was it must be a good thing to do. As smoking bans come into force in more and more places this social law is being interrupted and as such the habit is dying. However, with alcohol this powerful form of leverage is still very much a play. When I go into a bar or pub and ask for a soft drink the people who don't know me and don't know what I do for a living desperately want to know what's wrong and why I am not drinking. When I tell them that I don't drink there response is similar to what imagine people get when they announce they have something terminal. There faces are awash with great sadness and pity and they say things like 'oh how terrible for you'. It's a peculiar situation to get used to, but it is all part of the group insanity that alcohol creates.

Fighting the urge to drink when it is backed up by the law of social proof is like trying to arm-wrestle a gorilla. If your current social network includes an array of people who drink; trust me when I say, they absolutely do not want you to stop drinking. Why? Surely these people care about you and want you to succeed in hitting your personal goals and targets in life? Surely these friends understand you are taking a brave and difficult step towards better health and ensuring you will be around to see your children and eventually their children grow up?

Despite what these people feel about you, no matter how much love and empathy they have for you, they are still blinded by their own addiction. Remember, 80% of people who drink are no longer in control, granted, all to very varied levels along the path, but nonetheless we are all on the exact same path. All drinkers are sitting in the same mousetrap, stuffing their cheeks with cheese under the illusion that they are in control. In reality, the trap is in control and always was.

Human beings are motivated primarily on a selfish level and by just two component factors; the need to avoid pain and gain pleasure. I will go into much more detail about this later in the course, but for now I will explain it simply as this; if you introduce pain into someone's life they will subconsciously do absolutely everything possible to restore the balance. This does not necessarily mean that they will continue the forward momentum until they reach the point of experiencing pleasure; normally just going so far as to stop the pain is enough.

Deep down inside we all know that alcohol is exceptionally bad for us, all the signs are there, we just choose to ignore them. So when you stop drinking, you appear to raise your standards above those of the people around you. As you raise your own standards, you automatically highlight their low standards, and this causes psychological pain to everyone around you. You can replicate the phenomenon quite easily, simply go to a party where drinks are flowing and announce that you are going to drink water all night. I guarantee at least three or more guests will pounce on you like vampires in the blood bank. Watch how desperate they become for you to have a drink, they throw lines at you like "just have one little one" and "come on, lighten up, you only live once". If you are male, they may even question your sexuality. WHY? Why do well-meaning, kind-hearted individuals suddenly turn into schoolyard bullies when you stop drinking?

The answer is simple; they don't want you to remind them that what they are doing must one day also stop. Whether by choice or by a different, rather more unfortunate set of circumstances, it's easier for them to remove the pain (i.e. You and you uncomfortable highlighting of their weaknesses) than address their own problem in the first place, and human beings will almost always take the path of least resistance.

So, for this section I will remind you that if you lie down with dogs, you WILL get up with fleas. The next time you are in a pub and someone asks you if you want a drink and you reply "no" because you are not thirsty. As they laugh, throw insults and cajole you into reconsidering your blatant faux pas; remember you are the one on the higher ground looking down, not the other way around. They may be laughing and smiling as they point out your foolish error, but make no mistake, their need for you to drink is not for your benefit, it's purely to remove pain from their own situation.

Before I emigrated from the United Kingdom to Cyprus I tried to get a head start on my move to a foreign country by taking Greek lessons with a fantastic teacher called Linda Weaver from Warrington. Linda spent nearly twenty years living in Greece and even married a Greek man during her time there. She has a superb grasp of the language and is an accomplished and famous teacher of the subject. However, no matter how many lessons I had I could not get my head around the complexities of the native tongue of Cyprus, my future home. I believe the main reason I struggled is because my exposure to Greek was limited to the one hour a week I spent in Linda's conservatory having my lesson. Once I left her pretty suburban home I never heard another word of Greek until I arrived back on the same driveway a week or so later.

However, this embarrassingly remedial ability in the Greek language only seemed to apply when I was in the UK. Once in Cyprus I picked up phrases and vocabulary at a spectacular rate. After only a few weeks of residency I could have basic conversations with most people I came into contact with. Does being surrounded by the very things you aspire to be really make that much of an impact?

The answer is a massive 'yes'; it is the human ability to adapt that is as much the reason for our success as a species as it is an explanation for our failings. Put an Englishman in a foreign country and eventually he will become a local, absorbing the cultural differences and making them a part of his own personality. Unfortunately we are just as good as adapting to damaging and dangerous situations as we are to the positive traits around us. While the human body does not want to live in an environment where its host regularly consumes an addictive poison it will still adapt to this lifestyle out of pure determination to survive and thrive.

If drinkers surround you then you are in a 'drinking environment' and you will find this whole process slightly more difficult. Smokers who live with a partner who also smokes will find it more difficult to quit than someone who lives in a smoke free home. There is nothing you can do about other people so forget about trying to change those around you. Please do not even try to preach this message to your friends and colleagues – they don't want to hear it. The best counter balance to this problem is to also socialize in an environment of like-minded people. Hang out with other individuals who have also recognized the truth about alcohol and are starting out on a sober lifestyle. You will find these people in the forums of the Alcohol Lied to Me online club, my online community of people just like you – who have finally escaped the trap of alcohol addiction (www.StopDrinkingExpert.com) and they are always more than happy to help and support you on your journey.

You might think it strange that I tell you not to preach this message to other people. After all I am an author and I make my living out of the royalties from book sales, so why would I try and persuade you to keep this method a secret?

Alcohol is so firmly embedded into our collective conscious that when you stop drinking for good, you will observe some very strange situations. Actually, as I am writing this, one of those occasions has just conveniently arisen. I am typing this section of 'Alcohol Lied to Me' 37,000 feet over the French Alps on route from Manchester, England to Larnaca, Cyprus. As I boarded and took my seat, a familiar face greeted me. Andrea, a friend of mine who I have not seen for many years and now works for the airline. She just happens to be the senior cabin stewardess aboard this fight to Cyprus. It made me feel quite special to get a hug and kiss on the cheek from the airhostess as she took my ticket (that has certainly never happened before). As she hugged me, she whispered in my ear "don't worry, I will make sure you are looked after".

There was no room in first class, but she made sure I got special attention; I am sure to the annoyance of the other passengers seated nearby. I was moved to sit with a whole row of seats to myself, and not more than 30 minutes into the flight her colleague approached me and asked if I would like a complementary drink. I ordered a coffee. The same stewardess came back an hour later and asked if I would like something else and I ordered a fresh orange juice and some crisps, which she quickly and politely delivered to my seat with a smile. Not long after, Andrea came to see me herself, and with a confused expression on her face asked "do you not want some wine or whiskey?" I assured her I was fine and she gave me a smile as she dashed off to respond to another passenger who had pressed the call button.

About a third of the way through this five hour flight, I had already enjoyed a coffee, OJ, mineral water, a hot meal and now a Cola, all gratis, thanks to my friend the air hostess.

But something was wrong; Andrea sat in the empty seat next to me, "are you sure you don't want some wine?" she asked, and again I smiled back at her and said "I am fine". Her face crumpled with confusion, "are you driving as soon as you land, is that why you don't want it? You can take some bottles with you if you want," she added. I held a hand up to subconsciously emphasize the point and smiled again, "no Andrea, honestly I am fine, I don't need any wine". She nodded an "okay", smiled and walked back down the cabin, obviously perplexed by the strange man who didn't leap at the chance of free alcohol. As she walked away, I got the distinct impression I had offended her somehow. It couldn't have been because I had refused her generosity, because I had eaten and drank like a king for the first three hours of the flight and not paid a penny for the privilege.

In a society where 80% of people drink poison for apparently social reasons, this is the sort of event you will experience over and over again, especially when alcohol is offered free.

Turning down free poison appears to be one of the most offensive things you can do in polite society. This simple act appears to cause great discomfort and distrust for the person offering the booze. When you ask for a soft drink instead, they assure you that it isn't a problem, and yet they walk off to the fridge with the most disingenuous expression on their face you have ever seen.

How do you explain your sober lifestyle choice?

My advice to you is simply don't; you are not the one doing something wrong. I have found it is best to just avoid getting into explanations or reasons as to why you don't want alcohol. Don't feel the urge to churn out the old stalwart of "I am on antibiotics", because that just moves the interrogation a little further down the road, at some point you are going to find yourself in another social situation with the same person. The fact that you are considered the strange one because you don't want to ingest toxin is clear evidence of how twisted the collective thinking of society has become around this drug. In reality, it should be them explaining to you why they want to drink an addictive drug.

In all social situations around booze, firmly but politely turn down alcohol, you don't need to explain why you are not drinking, there is no need to make statements about being a teetotaler. You should never force your views about booze on other people. Honestly, this is a fruitless pursuit and a complete waste of time. It would be easier for you to sell double glazing to a man who lives in a tent... they simply don't want to buy what you are selling!

A friend of mine once told me that he doesn't trust people who don't drink! That is seriously impressive brainwashing you are witnessing there. 'Mr. Alcohol' stand up and take a bow, you have managed to programme 80% of the western world to believe it's the people who don't drink poison for fun who are the ones with the questionable judgment. If it weren't so sad, it should be considered manipulation psychology approaching degrees of pure genius. Imagine if MacDonald's could come up with a marketing campaign that worked so effectively that society went on to believe that it's the obese people who are not eating enough fast food!

Chapter Seven
Threshold Moments

Let's talk more about motivation and the theory that we are all enslaved to two basic driving desires: the need to avoid pain and gain pleasure. Everything in your life, at one level or another, is based on how it plays to these two primary needs. An easy example to illustrate this point is to ask you to take a good look at your body now, it's unlikely there is nothing about it you don't like or think could be improved. After all, we are all our own worst critics, and whether it's the general shape or size of your body, or there are more specific areas you are not comfortable with, there will undoubtedly be some areas which you would like to improve.

So the big question is, why don't you do something about it?

Why don't overweight people who are painfully unhappy with their size and shape, correct the problem? Why don't people who get out of breath running up a flight of stairs get on an exercise programme to improve their fitness? The answer is an internal belief that the application of the cure creates more pain than the eventual pleasure of succeeding in the goal.

Imagine an overweight individual who hates what they see when they look in the mirror, who gets depressed while clothes shopping because they struggle to find the designer clothes they want in their size. Can we agree that for that person slimming down and becoming that trim, fit and athletic person they dream of would be an absolutely amazing feeling?

It would bring enormous pleasure to anyone to be able to walk down the street and notice the admiring glances of passersby. To make any clothes look fantastic on their chiseled and defined torso. Surely such pleasure is worth the pain of dieting?

Judging by the escalating levels of chronic obesity, this does not appear to be the case.

In reality, human beings will do significantly more to avoid pain than they will do to gain pleasure. While it's undoubtedly true, having a super model body would bring great pleasure, the perceived journey to get there contains too much pain for most people to contemplate tolerating. So the result is that many people remain in a perpetual limbo period with most things in their life that they are not satisfied with. They are not totally happy with the amount of money they earn, but prefer to hang in a mediocre position than suffer the initial pain of pushing through their comfort zone to become a more skilled, talented, and experienced or specialist employee. How many people remain in a dead-end job daydreaming of their own business that they would love to set up but NEVER do anything about it?

The same rule applies to alcohol; you know deep down inside you would be happier without poison flushing around in your system on a daily basis. You know you would have more money in your pocket, more time awake and less time crashed out in a drunken paralysis.

You know how wonderful it would feel to not care if you have a drink today or not, so why don't you deal with it? Simple… because at the moment you associate more pain with removing alcohol than you associate pleasure with stopping drinking.

Because of the ever-changing needs and demands of the ego, this perception of what constitutes pleasure and pain is always shifting. The most likely reason that you purchased this book is that you encountered what I call a 'Threshold Moment'. Essentially, something happened that temporally altered the balance of the scales. This is an event so traumatic that it causes an unbearable amount of pain that sends you into a massive determined period of change. Let me give you a few examples of threshold moments in relation to drinking before I give you my own:

Life is cruising along nicely in your usual blinkered and ironic state, where you are acutely aware that you are drinking far too much and probably doing serious damage to your health, career and loved ones, and yet you still reach for the bottle of wine every night as soon as you get home. Happy to ignore all the warning signs in favor of blind ignorance.

One night... You are sitting watching television, your ego sedated and comfortably numb by the glass of mild anesthetic grasped comfortably in your hand. Your five-year-old daughter comes up to you with a carefully and proudly drawn picture. It's a colorful drawing of you, her daddy. You are slumped in front of the television and in your hand a bottle of wine! BANG, Suddenly it hits you like a tonne of bricks – this is how your own child sees you. Through her pure, innocent eyes she see you for the real addict that you are. Children have no binding compulsion to pull any punches or to spare your feelings; they just tell it how it is.

Children are blank canvasses and they learn in their formative years solely by watching us, the grown ups. This social pleasantry that has made us so utterly miserable is here now because it has been passed down through the generations as a curse wrapped up in shiny paper and labeled as a gift.

The reason this book gets updated annually is because every year thousands more people use it to help them stop drinking. Many of them send me their stories and the collective wisdom of all us ex-drinkers is worth more than the sum of their parts. This is a heartbreaking story I was emailed only this week from Linda (not her real name as she has asked to remain anonymous). Linda grew up with an alcoholic mother and later went onto to have her own struggle with drink until she joined my online club last year. If you are a parent and wonder how your drinking effects your children Linda's story is difficult but vital for you to read:

Being brought up by my alcoholic mother has had a profound effect on my own self-perception and my relationship with alcohol.

My childhood is a combination of good vs bad but alcohol made the world around me evil. I was protected from nothing and exposed to all as a result of having no parents to shelter me. Alcohol made my childhood a living nightmare - it took away the amazing, loving, proud mother I had and gave me a women that I was mortified to be associated with.

I remember seeing her tears, her worries over money, anxiety in social situations and what was the answer? Alcohol. That was her answer each time, no matter the devastation caused by the last binge. She was so embroiled in the vicious pattern that she couldn't be a mother. I grew up being able to do whatever I wanted and there were no consequences for my actions as my mum was a drunk - she would turn up drunk to formal meetings with my principle but then forget the conversation so I got away with everything. This all accumulated in to a general lack of respect I had for anyone, even myself. I respected no one and listened to no one know - no one cared for me, after all if your own parents can't be there for you, who can? More than a lack of respect for others, I didn't respect or love myself, my mother never took time to emotionally invest in me which left me feeling unworthy of love, so I rebelled to get the attention I craved.

My mother's drinking took her away from me - she didn't see the child I was, she didn't acknowledge my achievements, and she didn't attend my sporting events - all because alcohol got in the way. I was dragged up in a world no child should have to witness.

When she wasn't drinking she was the mum I loved and the best mother on planet earth - she would apologize, have a movie day, buy us sweets, and tell us it would never happen again...but the pattern continued.

As a result of my upbringing, I went through a decade of my life unable to have a few drinks with my friends, I went from entering the bar to being paralytic as I had no control over my drinks. The way I have been brought up is you drink until your unconscious - there is no middle ground. It took years to bring this behavior under control and even now alcohol scares me.

I lost my childhood and so much more because of my mother's addiction to alcohol, I would not wish any child to experience the life I did with my mum.

Regardless of the world she brought me up in, I still love her as I know somewhere inside she is still there...but alcohol has won this battle, I only hope it won't win the war too!

Linda, United Kingdom

Whether you have your own child's super honest portrait of you pinned to the refrigerator door or perhaps Linda's story made you question your own behavior, these sorts of events can be considered for many to be what I call a threshold moment, an event so powerfully painful that it forces you to change. The 'pain versus pleasure' scales take a dramatic nudge in one direction, and your perception of what you are doing changes enough for you to take action. Normally people on the road to giving up Attractively Packaged Poison have several increasingly severe threshold moments along the way.

Let me tell you what my own personal threshold moment was like:

I am wonderfully blessed, and it could be said I have been guilty in the past of not appreciating that fact. I could be accused of being fantastically blaze about my two wonderful children who are 11 and 7. Without a modicum of ego here, I can tell you they look at me like I am faultless. I could have lived up to that view much better without alcohol distracting me from the true beauty of the gift I had been consecrated with.

I can't tell you how many fun days out there could have been that I never permitted to happen, just because I could not see a way for the day to include alcohol. I don't want to torture myself by considering how many options I took purely because they included alcohol. Option A might have been more fun for my children and option C might have been more enjoyable for my wife, but in the past, if option B included alcohol then that was always the only choice I took, because I couldn't see how anything could be enjoyable without a drink.

At this point I will remind you that while I am sharing this with you, I don't believe in beating yourself up with your mistakes of the past. The past is very important in as much as it brought you to where you are now, but it has absolutely no relevance on tomorrow. Just because I made bad decisions in the past, does not mean I am compelled to make them again now, tomorrow or at any point in the future. Every dawn brings an exciting new opportunity for you to get it right. Trust me, I know you are at the start of a tough journey, but the commitment you have made just investing your money in this book (money you could quite have easily spent on your favorite brand of booze) is a dramatic and profound statement of intent.

Remember, as Woody Allen says "80% of success is just turning up", so if you are here as the result of a painful threshold moment, don't let that pain subside enough for you to believe that purchasing this book is enough to make a difference. Absorb it over and over; use the subliminal tools available from my website to help you alter your programming around alcohol.

Every time you observe the ego and catch it in the act of attempting to take over control of your choices, you reduce its power by a fraction of one percent. If you consistently keep doing this over time, I know the future is bright. Every day is worth living, and if you don't believe me about that right here and now, just try missing one of them!

When I became a dad I was determined to be closer to my children than my own dad was with me. I would always be there; I would be the kind of dad that they could always turn to no matter what. I would be the father who took his son fishing and his daughter to see the latest pop concert. My children and my wife would be safe, secure and happy. They would never have to worry about bills or whether we could afford this or that, I would work as hard as I needed to just to make it happen. What I never considered in this grand plan was what would happen if you took me out of the equation. What if I was not around to provide for and protect my family?

In 1997 I had to consider that situation could be a very real and likely possibility.

At this point I was drinking in the region of two bottles of wine a day; of course, I was still lying to myself profusely. I figured that because I had no urge to drink first thing in the morning, and my drinking in no way affected my work, I could not be an alcoholic. If I am honest, I didn't and still don't like the word alcoholic. For me it describes the guy lying in the gutter swilling cheap whiskey from a brown paper bag, not me. I could not possibly have a serious drink problem; I was a director of two companies and had just been appointed to the board of a children's charity. And yet, every evening as soon as I got home I opened the first bottle of wine and gulped the first half down like it was the first gasp of oxygen to a free diver returning from the depths of the deep blue. By the time I fell into bed the second bottle would be empty, perhaps I would throw away the last mouthful just so if my wife asked I would honestly say that I had not had a full two bottles of wine.

I consider myself to be a relatively intelligent person, and yet here I was throwing a mouthful of wine away just so I could face my spouse and lie with a free conscience. It's amazing how tunnel-visioned we become, how we ignore the unnatural behavior we should recognize as warning signs.

At the height of my own problem I couldn't even contemplate a night at the movies without a drink. Movie theatres are full of popcorn, sweets and super sized buckets of fizzy drinks, but rarely can you take an alcoholic drink into the movie. This was a problem for me (although it seemed normal at the time), after a hard day at work I didn't think it was fair that I should be deprived of my evening drink by a movie. I would sometimes buy a quarter bottle of whiskey and pour it into one of those 'big gulp' colas and sip on it all the way through the film.

Once alcohol takes hold of you, it never lets go. The grip is always tightened, I can't remember when I started drinking in movie theatres but it didn't phase me. Alcohol moves so slowly that you don't even notice how deep you are sinking. I hope you stay with me to the end of the book but regardless please never assume your situation will get better on its own. If you ignore the problem now, it can only get worse.

This was my threshold moment!

In January 1997 after a particularly heavy festive season, I started to get a dull ache in my right abdomen just under my right rib. I dismissed it as a hundred different minor, insignificant medical problems from a bit of food poisoning to an intolerance of wheat; I even considered paying £300 for a food allergy blood test. In summary, I considered everything apart from the obvious, that the 140 units of alcohol a week were destroying my insides the same way alcohol destroys all life at a cellular level.

In February 1997, the dull ache was preventing me getting to sleep and I started searching the internet for my symptoms. As I scanned the possible reasons for a pain in this region I suddenly became genuinely scared. Website after website suggested liver cancer, liver failure, liver cirrhosis, pancreatic failure, alcohol induced gall bladder disease. The lists went on and on, all horrific illnesses, all caused by alcohol, and many were irreversible. I made an appointment to see my doctor.

In my lifetime I have never had anything seriously wrong with me; I have only ever been to the doctor for a cold or simple chest infection. My past experiences with the medical profession mean I always confidently expect to be told that the condition will clear up on its own, or that a short dose of antibiotics would be all that is needed. This time was different.

I sat in the doctor's waiting room, shaking with fear. I walked in and explained my symptoms. He asked how much I was drinking, I lied and said I used to drink a lot but now I have no more than a glass of wine a night. Can you believe that even at this point I still lied? Of course you can – you still do it all the time! This is the power of this drug we freely hand out to children at celebrations as a 'treat' to make them feel grown up. In honest fear for my life, face to face with a medical professional who was there to help me, I still lied to protect my opportunity to drink. Despite the fact that it was slowly killing me, I couldn't cope with the possibility that it would be taken away from me, so I lied to the doctor.

If you are not from the United Kingdom, let me explain that doctors in England are normally seen at the cost of the state on the National Health Service. Doctor's surgeries are usually over-subscribed and getting an appointment is sometimes difficult. My allocated time with Dr White was five minutes, behind me there were another seven patents all waiting for their own five minutes. After 35 minutes of examinations and questions, I knew this was going to be a very different experience than I was used to at the doctors.

I still expected, even after all the fuss, for the doctor to nod reassuringly and say "well, I've checked you over and you seem fine, come back in a month if it doesn't improve". Dr White had a concerned but kind face, he looked up from his notes over his small round glasses and said "there is a very real possibility there is something serious behind your pain. I don't have the facilities here to examine you to the level I need to, so I am having you sent to the gastroenterology department at the hospital".

Hospital! Surely not! That is where sick people go; the health service is overstretched as it is, surely they wouldn't waste a valuable bed on someone young and healthy like me? As I walked home, neither cured nor reassured, this was the point when I realized this was not a figment of my imagination. I had possibly seriously damaged my body by selfishly drinking my attractively packaged poison.

I sat at home and watched my children play, and it felt like my heart had been ripped out. Knowing how much I love my family, how could I do that to them? How could I leave my children with out a daddy? How could I be so selfish that I would make my children go through the pain of watching their dad's funeral? How could I be so pathetic that I would risk making my wife a single parent, with two devastated children to look after and no income? I am not ashamed to tell you my world was ripped apart that evening, and I cried myself to sleep in a world of self-pity, regret and guilt.

This was my ultimate threshold moment; it altered the balance of all things. For a brief time the pain of continuing to drink was greater than the pain of living without my drug. I stopped drinking for eight weeks and the pain subsided a little. The hospital performed dozens of blood tests and scans, and I was awaiting a liver biopsy because my enzymes were all over the place (a clear indication that my liver was in trauma). The problem with relying on a threshold event to cure your problem is, as soon as the pain generated by the threshold begins to fade, your determination to stick to your goals fades too, and you're back in the hands of good old-fashioned will-power. Let me tell you here and now, will-power is no friend of yours or mine.

Will-power is civil war, because it breaks a human need rule, it breaks the law of scarcity. I will explain in greater depth about this later in the course, but for the moment, if you want proof that you are fighting a losing battle trying to stop drinking with will-power, let me prove it to you.

The classic self help process that relies on will-power is dieting. When you look in the mirror and decide you need to shed some weight, as soon as you start restricting the amount of food you are allowed, the body goes into shock. Suddenly the subconscious assumes there is a drastic shortage of food. This scenario is in direct conflict with your primary functional need 'to stay alive at all costs'.

The brain, thinking you are in the middle of a famine, starts applying pressure in the form of pain to get you to reverse the situation. Subconsciously you are in preservation mode; it is irrelevant that you want to lose weight or indeed that it may even be beneficial for you to drop a dress size or two. Your subconscious does not rationalize, it just completes tasks. This is why 95% of people who go on a calorie restrictive diet not only put the weight back on within five years, but have on average added an additional five pounds.

So the threshold pain faded and I was left with nothing but will-power... I started drinking again, but this time I had a new system. Alcohol is a creative little poison and had come up with a brilliant new way for me to carry on flirting with her at a new, safe level. I bought a lockable drinks cabinet and loaded it with single measure bottles of whiskey, I gave the key to my wife and explained that I was only allowed one measure a night, and if I asked for more she was to say no. It worked well for a whole week, well worth the £250 that the cabinet cost. The plan fell down when my wife went out with friends for an evening and she took the key with her. I felt cheated because I had not even had a single drink, and she was breaking the rules; I was allowed one a day... how dare she do this to me!

I was like a petulant child, it didn't take me long to realize that the back of the cabinet was made of cheap plywood and was only tacked into place. A simple bit of leverage with a steak knife and the panel lifted up enough to squeeze a small bottle out. The new plan was dead from this point on!

Within three weeks the pain was back and stronger than ever, and more tests eventually revealed that if I didn't want to risk liver failure within two to three years, I had to stop drinking immediately. I stopped drinking... for three weeks, and started again. Even faced with a death sentence I still couldn't see how giving up booze was a life worth living.

I can't order you to stop drinking, your wife or husband screaming at you won't stop you drinking, your children begging you, still won't make you see sense. Even YOU grasping the nettle and deciding to give up and resist temptation is futile. The only way you can live without this drug is to fundamentally change your opinion of it. You need to see it for what it really is: 'attractively packaged poison'. You have probably tried to give up or cut down in the past and failed, this is because at the end of the day you still want it, need it and desire it. You still believe that alcohol is in some way benefiting you.

I have heard every excuse going from people just like you and just like me:

- I can't sleep without a drink before bed
- I need it to relax
- I am boring without a drink
- Drinking gives me confidence
- It helps me chill out after a hard days work

These are all lies, and deep down inside you know they are, if you are currently using any of these statements, from now on see them as evidence that you are currently sitting inside a giant mousetrap resolutely believing you are perfectly safe.

The day you stop seeing alcohol as a benefit and seeing it for what it really is, you will start to become free. As you work with me during this book you will slowly begin to become aware that alcohol no longer tastes as good as it used to. You will start noticing the unpleasant taste that you have previously learned to ignore (often people report a strange sensation of disappointment with their drink). The harshness of the poison will slowly become more and more dominant over the heaps of sugar and fruit the drinks companies use to disguise the drug hidden within. It may sound unbelievable to you at this point, but using my system you will get to the point where you find the taste of alcoholic drinks unappealing, disappointing and often just plain disgusting (just like you did when you first took a sneaky sip of your father's beer when you were younger).

In the interest of honesty, I will forewarn you of my intention to use a sneaky persuasion technique on you called a 'pre-supposition'. Salesmen use these types of questions to appear to be offering you a choice, when in actual fact all the responses serve the same purpose. A good example of a pre-supposition that might have been used on you as a young child (perhaps unwittingly) by your parents would be "do you want to go to bed now or in ten minutes time?" The question appears to give you the luxury of a choice, but all outcomes result in the same thing – you in bed within ten minutes.

My sneaky question to you is; do you want to stop drinking completely or just cut down a bit and repeat this course every time you lose control again until you stop? Obviously I am trying to gently push you in the direction I know you should go, and despite telling you the option to cut down has repeated failure built into it, your ego still thinks it is in control and can handle anything. Be certain of this, your ego doesn't want you to stop drinking because it predicts that will result in pain/fear in the future.

I know many readers would prefer to cut down rather than stop, but the only logical solution is for you to step out of the mousetrap and never get back in. If you are dependent upon alcohol and you don't want to stop, you have not quite grasped the problem. If a heroin addict came up to you and said "I have decided to only use drugs on a Tuesday and never any other day", how confident are you that if you bumped into him again in a years time that would be still the case. Alcoholism is a binary condition, it is either on or off, you can't be a little bit alcoholic in the same way you can't be a little bit pregnant!

You may need to read this book over and over before you get to this point and your decision is in harmony with my advice. Stopping completely really is the best option for you, but you must come to that decision on your own.

You can't be convinced by me, your family or friends and nobody can order you to take this stance, it has to come deep from within you. If you don't currently feel like that, if you are still at the point where you believe you can control the situation, or that you enjoy it too much to stop completely, don't panic or beat yourself up too much. You are not alone in this struggle in my online community you will find people who are in exactly the same position as you. Nobody has ever developed a drink problem and then woke up the next morning and cured it in a eureka moment of perfection.

Part of the journey to sobriety is experiencing the futility of trying to find a way to keep the bits you like while removing the consequences you don't want. It is like trying to bail out the Titanic with a bucket; for a while you may believe you are making headway, but very soon you start to see that you can't possibly succeed. I tried dozens and dozens of different buckets before I came to the realization that the good parts of drinking go hand in hand with the bad, and you can't have one without the other.

Here are just a few of the buckets I thought might bail out my sinking ship:

- I will only drink at the weekends.
- I will only drink socially and never at home.
- I will drink a glass of water for every glass of alcohol I drink.
- I will take three months off the drink each year.
- I will only drink beer and no wine or spirits.
- I will only drink wine and with food as part of a meal.

Add to that list of ridiculous theories the expensive prescription drugs I turned to. The first I tried was Disulfiram, which interferes with the way your liver processes alcohol and makes you violently ill if you drink. The problem with this drug is that it relies on your discipline to take it every morning (alcoholics are not renowned for their discipline). Initially, if I knew there was a big party or social occasion I was going to, I just wouldn't take it (and so begins the failure routine). Predictably I then loosened my rules further by only taking it Monday to Friday, allowing myself to drink at the weekends, I convinced myself that I deserved a treat at the weekends for being so good during the week.

The next stage of my defiance came when I resented the drug preventing me from drinking during the week and I experimented with it and found that I could just about tolerate a small beer while taking it. Any more than that and the side effects would knock me flat on my back. One night I pushed it a little further and had a large beer and a glass of wine. Within twenty minutes my head was pounding, my face blushing bright red, while my heart felt like it was trying to beat its way out of my chest cavity. For a moment I honestly thought I might die, and the only solution was to lie in a dark room motionless for several hours until the effects subsided.

I tried other drugs, such as Acamprosate Calcium, which interfere with the release of dopamine, essentially taking all the pleasure out of drinking. Over time it renders your favorite tipple as pleasurable as a soft drink, and logically you only want to drink one of those when you are thirsty. Again, with this drug the will-power or discipline required to take a daily tablet that ruins the very thing you are addicted to is a significant challenge. Add to that some pretty horrendous side effects from dizzy spells, insomnia, dry mouth and worse, and you start to think that feeling this bad to stay off the drink is simply not worth it.

Whether it's crazy routines or pills, they are all simply evidence of the ego's delusion that it is in some way in control. All these method use some form of will-power that can't possibly work, because underneath the smoke screen you still believe that alcohol is a benefit that you are being deprived of.

Remember, there is no such thing as failure, things that go wrong are just events in the past, a time period we are no longer concerned with. If you finish reading this book and go three weeks without a drink and then slip up, the natural temptation (and the ego's opinion) is to think that this book doesn't work, you are not strong enough, or you are destined to always be a problem drinker. Recognize this belief for what it is; the conscious mind trying to predict the future – a skill it simply doesn't have. If you fall off the wagon… big deal, dust yourself down and carry on. When you wake in the morning, what is the point of beating yourself up about that mistake you made the night before? The past no longer exists.

Presumably you haven't woken up with a bottle in your hand having been drinking in your sleep somehow, so right there in that moment (where all of life is lived), you are not a drinker. Equally, now that we know that the future also doesn't exist and will never exist, the fact that you had a drink the night before has no bearing on whether you will have one later that day, tomorrow, the next day or ever again. Take each moment as it comes, every second that you decide you don't want to drink is a success.

The secret to stopping drinking is the same as the secret to get anything else in life that you want, and this is to remain in the moment. Don't make predictions about what sort of person you will be in the future. I wouldn't ask you to predict what will happen tomorrow anymore than I would ask you to perform open heart surgery on me, you simply don't have the skills to help me (of course, I am recklessly playing the numbers here, one day this book will land with an eminent heart surgeon and he will be mortally offended by that statement). Your journey out of the mousetrap happens by being aware of our egoic mind; every time you find your mind wandering into the future or past, observe this happening from the point of view of an outsider. Disconnect yourself from the process; catch your ego at work.

For your conscious mind to have any power at all, it needs you to believe that you and it are one and the same thing. If you see if for what it really is; a minor part of your mind at work then it loses all its influence over you. Every time you catch your mind starting to worry, predict or reflect on past events and deliberately pull yourself back into the present moment you reduce its power over you by a fraction of one percent.

For most people the conscious mind seizes control of them tens of thousands of times a day, and so this process isn't a magic bullet cure. I can't promise if you do this ten times, twenty times or fifty times you will be cured, but then you didn't become alcohol dependent overnight, and no system out there can hope to restore the correct balance in a similar brief time period. Most other detox systems require a period of withdrawal, often called going 'cold turkey', which for an alcoholic is at best torturous, and in worst case scenarios can be fatal.

My method starts with your deep-seated desire to end this painful cycle and slowly deconstructs the obstacles preventing you from achieving your goal. Slowly, over time, as you keep resisting the attempted hijackings by your egoic mind you will feel a sense of peace begin to build. Once you get beyond the physical dependence on alcohol, your urge to drink is generated by the wants and needs of the ego, as this reduces so does your desire for alcohol.

A popular question at this point is "how long will it take?" I can't predict the future any more than you can, so won't even try to give you a specific prediction. For most people, once they understand that everything they previously believed about alcohol being a benefit was a big fat lie and can see that a chemical imbalance is causing pain for their ego to respond to, they simply stop. For a great many people that is directly after reading this book, others need a few weeks for the information to sink in, and others read the book several times before the penny drops.

Whether it takes a day or a year is irrelevant, you will find this simple process will not only remove your damaging patterns around alcohol, but also all other negative habits too. Denying the ego will slowly repair everything from relationships to finances, if you want to go into greater detail about how it works then I would suggest you read my books 'Swallow The Happy Pill' and "The God Enigma'.

Once your conscious mind begins to loosen its grip on your perception of reality, this system becomes easier and easier. The secret to success is to stick at this long enough to become aware of a shift in power. So for the next 21 days I am going to ask you to commit to doing four things everyday. This does not mean after 21 days you are no longer dependent on alcohol, or that you can stop and return to your old ways. I just know if you diligently follow the four steps I will reveal as we continue through this book, for that amount of time you will start to see something amazing happen in your life.

Chapter Nine
The Cost Of Drinking

Have you added it up?:

Be honest how much do you spend on alcohol in an average day. Most people are shocked at how much money they are wasting on booze.

1 Bottle of averagely priced wine per day?
2 pints of lager (pub lunch)
  $9.99 per bottle / $4.00 per pint

Quit and you save:

$132.00 per week
$531.00 per month
$6380.00 per year

People who have a problem with alcohol usually significantly under estimate the amount they are drinking. Often making statements like 'I only have one glass of wine with my lunch'... but some red wine glasses can comfortably hold half a bottle of wine! Be honest with yourself and discover the true cost of your habit:

Day	$10.00	$12.50	$15.00	$17.50	$20.00	$22.50
Week	$70	$87	$105	$122	$140	157
Month	$280	$387	$465	$542	$620	$706
Year	$3360	$4562	$5475	$6387	$7300	$8478
Decade	$33600	$45620	$54750	$63870	$73000	$84780

When I stopped drinking I sat down and worked out how much I had been spending on booze. It's no surprise to me now that I didn't conduct this exercise while I was still drinking. I simply didn't want to hear the financial cost of my habit. I didn't want to hear any negatives about booze (this is pure ostrich syndrome), the same technique that stopped me going to the doctor because I was afraid he would tell me to stop drinking.

Western society acts as though alcohol is nothing more than a social pleasantry to be enjoyed with friends, but in reality it is a drug so powerful it can even prevent intelligent individuals from getting urgent medical help. Make no bones about it; this is a very dangerous and sinister drug – the ultimate wolf in sheep's clothing!

At the peak of my drinking I was knocking back two bottles of wine a night, plus a bottle of whiskey over the weekend. At a rough guess that equates to a daily spend on alcohol of $23.00 per day. A weekly spend of $161.00 or $724.00 every month. Wow! No wonder I didn't want to see this figure while I was still drinking, that would have shocked and depressed me – BUT, it still wouldn't have stopped me drinking, and that is perhaps the scariest thought of all.

If I hadn't stopped drinking, it's entirely likely I would have continued consuming booze at that ungodly rate, or even increased it further to compensate for my growing tolerance to the effects of the drug. This means that over the next decade (if I had lived that long) I would have blown $86,940 on my addiction. Even this startling admission is only a half-truth, because it doesn't allow for any of those ridiculously priced $400 bottles of 'art', Christmas, Birthdays or any other formal excuse to get excessively drunk.

I was spending nearly $9000 a year on drinking a poison while telling my children and family that we couldn't afford the expensive vacations or other little luxuries that we might have actually been able to have if I wasn't lying to them, and of course, to myself. Hopefully, as you are starting to see, alcohol misled me. It lied to me, and it continues to lie to you – the challenge I throw down to you now is 'what are you going to do about it?"

I encourage you to honestly do this exercise for yourself and calculate how much money you are spending on a common drug addiction. You will no doubt come up with an amount of money, which you can think of a hundred different and better things to spend it on. Sadly the financial cost is almost insignificant when compared to the other factors that need to be considered when you try to take stock of what alcohol has stolen from you.

Booze affects everyone differently, but for me it made me sleepy. In a practical sense, what this meant for me is when I got home from work at let's say 6pm; the first glass of wine was poured by 6.05pm. Less than an hour later first bottle was gone. By 8pm I had moved onto, and consumed about two thirds of the second bottle of wine (I would never drink the full second bottle because then I claim I had not drunk two full bottles of wine if anyone asked). At this point in the evening, after nearly two bottles of wine I could hardly keep my eyes open. I would spend the next 30 minutes staring at the clock wishing it were later so I could go to bed at a decent time. It would be rare for me to make it to 9pm, normally collapsing unconscious into bed between 8.30pm and 8.45pm.

I would sleep badly, waking several times to use the toilet and a few more times gasping for water to deal with the dehydration. My bloodshot eyes would blink open at 6am and I would head to work exhausted.

This was my life for longer than I care to admit, and while alcohol may not have the same outcome for you, there will almost certainly be another negative side effect to replace it. In my case, let's say a more reasonable bedtime for a 9 to 5 office worker is around 11pm. This means that my drinking took me offline for an additional 17 hours per week. Over ten years I spent 9,100 hours knocked out, unconscious because of my drug addiction. That time I will never get back, how many opportunities and experiences can you fit into nearly 10,000 hours?

The mind boggles.

The situation is even bleaker because I am a father; it's not just my time I was throwing away. Allow me to expand on this point to really ram home the gloomy message of what my drinking did:

If you are a parent I apologize for what I am about to ask you to do next. If you are visual or kinesthetic character type then this may be traumatic and painful for you to imagine, but please bear with me because I am doing this not to be cruel or give you nightmares, but rather to make a valuable point. Imagine for me; that tomorrow your child is abducted and you never see them again. Immediately such a horrific suggestion may remind you of what happened to the McCann family while on vacation in sunny Portugal a few years ago.

On Thursday 3rd May 2007, Jerry and Kate McCann put their little daughter Madeline to bed for the last time. At some point before midnight she was taken from her bed and has never been seen since.

If that happened to you and there was absolutely nothing you could do to prevent it happening, let me ask you, what price would you put on an hour spent with your daughter? If a few months later it were possible to buy the opportunity to see your child again and spend just one hour with them, what would you be prepared to pay?

Is it $1000, $10,000, $100,000 or is it priceless? Would you pay everything you had just to spend that one-hour with your child? I know for me the answer is the latter, and yet alcohol (the social drug) made me throw away over 9,000 hours that I could have spent with my lovely children Jordan and Aoife.

My children are the most precious things in my life, and yet a drug that people insist is just a bit of harmless fun, a beverage that they say is vital to the success of a party, a drink they demand must be consumed or you will be labeled boring and weird... Somehow this 'innocent' substance made me willingly give away 758 priceless days with my children.

I am going to take a break from writing at this point because I am so angry and feel so cheated that I don't think I can continue.

I will close this chapter by giving you one question to think about. What has alcohol stolen from you?

Is it your health, your time, your promotion, your money, your wife, your husband, your career? It may be one thing or it might be many, but as sure as night follows day, make no mistake about it... you are the victim of a serious theft. Unless you wake up and realize that the bottle of booze you thought was your friend is actually your worse enemy, then you will be a victim tomorrow, the day after and every day until the truth dawns on you.

The average drinker who joins my online stop drinking club is spending around $3000 a year on alcohol! That might sounds a lot, and the tendency of any drinker is to assume they are nowhere near that amount. But $3000 is less than ten bucks a day and so if you are one of those people who drink a bottle of wine a day plus a bit more at the weekend then you are way over that figure. Let's keep the glass half full (excuse the pun) and we will stick with the average. Every person I have ever spoken to has agreed that they could find something important to do with $3000 dollars.

If I gave you that money today and told you to go blow it, what would you do with it?

- Maybe take the kids to Disneyland?
- Put it towards a new car?
- A romantic vacation?
- Put it towards the college fund?
- A medical bill or procedure?
- Pay off a credit card?

Whether you would use it to make life bearable or to simply add pleasure for you and those you love. That money is there and waiting for you to do any one of those things. You don't have to ask your boss for a raise, work overtime or change job – it is already yours! To get it, all you have to do is step outside your current situation and see that alcohol is not your friend, helping you deal with a difficult life but rather your enemy, deliberately stealing all those wonderful things from you and your family.

My challenge to you is to put this book down and do the exercise that 95% of drinkers refuse to even consider. Sit down and honestly work out how much you spend on alcohol in a year. Make sure you include those lunchtime drinks with clients, weekend binges and the special occasions such as Christmas and birthdays. Those times when you treat yourself to much more expensive poison than usual. Come up with you golden number and then think about what you would do with that money if somebody gave it to you in a lump sum today.

Next take that image, whether it is the trip to Florida you have always wanted to take or clearing the debt that just won't leave you alone. Get on the Internet and find an image that represents that aspirational item. Print it out and stick it on the refrigerator or bathroom mirror. Somewhere where you will see it everyday. If you ever take that image down without having completed the goal you will know that alcohol still has a hold over you.

Chapter Ten
Supplementing the imbalance

Warning: Do not take any supplements listed here without consulting your doctor or other health care professional.

I am assuming you came to this book with a desire to stop drinking but were not quite sure how to go about it. I am hoping by now that desire has intensified, you now see booze for what it really is, and you are determined never to drink that foul tasting, life destroying poison that is alcohol again. If you are still hoping to go back to drinking one day, or are planning just to cut down, let me explain why that is a very bad idea.

All addictive drugs have what is known as a kick, the period after you stop taking them in which the side effects occur. Luckily for you, we are talking about an alcohol kick here, which is relatively mild compared to other street drugs. The reason heroin is so difficult to get off is because the kick is so intense and painful that the user has to endure agony knowing that all the pain could be made to vanish in a split second by just taking another hit of the drug.

Alcohol withdrawal begins from the moment you take your last sip, and will reach its peak intensity between 24 and 48 hours later. This is why many people become evening drinkers, and the first thing they do when they get home after a hard day at work is reach for the bottle opener. As they arrive home they are exactly mid-way through the most powerful phase of the withdrawal process. Alcohol withdrawal is so subtle that we are unable to identify the symptoms unless we are aware of what to look for. Withdrawal from booze feels like a general feeling of unease, to the everyday person it may feel a little like stress or anxiety. This is why people incorrectly claim that a drink when they get home from work helps them unwind. The only thing that first drink does is turn off the withdrawal symptoms of the previous days drinking. So to a certain extent it's true; they do feel instantly less stressed, because the general unease and anxiety directly created by the alcohol has now gone, but if they hadn't drank the day before, it wouldn't have been there in the first place. So all you are fixing is the previous day's mistake.

The full chemical withdrawal from alcohol, regardless of the amount you drink, lasts around two weeks, climbing to a climax around 36 hours after the last drink and slowly fading away to near zero after a couple of weeks. Because of the hard wiring you have constructed in your brain, and your overactive hypothalamus, you may never achieve total zero, but everyday you don't drink, the base state of withdrawal drops a little further.

If you are currently dependent upon alcohol to the point where if you stop you experience traumatic physical symptoms such as spasms, fitting, fever and vomiting, you will need to see your doctor and explain that you are using this method to stop. Your general practitioner will be able to give you prescription medication to help suppress these unpleasant side effects while you go through the kick.

This extended withdrawal period is exactly why you cannot safely have 'just one drink', that one drink is the reason why 95% of people trying to quit with 'will-power' fail. One sip of alcohol may take less than five seconds to consume, but will start an unstoppable process that will last at least two weeks. During that period a new chemical imbalance will force you to crave another drink and that pain will only stop for two reasons. Firstly, the discomfort will go away if you take a drink of alcohol, and secondly, that pain will dissipate if you give it long enough. So in summary, the only way to stop the pain of an alcohol kick is to drink or to not drink. Only one of those solutions doesn't create another problem the next day, and I don't need to tell you which one.

If for the briefest moment you start to think 'just one drink won't do any harm' or 'I will only have one glass of wine with my evening meal', you are willingly stepping back into the mousetrap and assuming that this time you are safe, one more poke at the cheese won't make any difference!

You drink because there is a chemical imbalance in your brain, but the catch 22 is that while the alcohol gives you a short-term release from the imbalance by flooding the brain with more of the chemicals you crave. Withdrawal from alcohol also causes a chemical imbalance all of its own. So now you have two problems; one created by the booze, and one that was there in the first place. The discomfort of the first imbalance makes you create the second imbalance and you get trapped in a never-ending loop.

So here is how you break the loop once and for all. Firstly, stop drinking, I mean today... right now. Unlike before when you have had this brave moment we are going to do something vitally different, we are going to stop the first imbalance from triggering the second imbalance. Remember, for the next two weeks you may feel uneasy, uncomfortable and anxious, this is caused by the kick from alcohol, an addictive drug. The good news is once you get 14 to 15 days sober, the symptoms are so mild you can't distinguish them from the genuine emotions of daily life.

This time when you quit we are not going to leave you at the mercy of your imbalanced brain chemistry. We know one of the most important substances for proper brain function, and by that I mean having correctly functioning neuro transmitters and receptors, is essential fats in the brain. If you have ever spilt oil or fat on a piece of fabric you will know that water won't even touch it. To get rid of an oil stain you need to add a chemical solvent to break it down. You won't be surprised to hear that one solvent that is particularly good at this job is alcohol. While this is good news if you need to rescue an expensive sofa with a nasty oil stain, it is very bad news for us problem drinkers. Alcohol destroys essential fat; it rips through it like napalm.

As a heavy drinker you almost certainly have an essential fat deficiency, and this means your receptors cannot function correctly. This problem means that when your body creates the dopamine and serotonin that make you feel good; you are going to struggle to absorb them at a sufficient level to be noticeable.

Can you now see that if you understand the truth about alcohol, are free of the kick and feel great within yourself (because the dopamine and serotonin is pumping naturally around your body), there is very little chance you will even want to drink, and so you don't. If you have given up the drink but feel terrible and depressed you are obviously more likely to assume it is the alcohol that was making life bearable and return to it as a solution to your problem.

The two specific essential fats that we need to take onboard at the point where we stop drinking are Eicosapentaenoic Acid and Docosahexaenoic Acid. Known better simply as EHA and DHA, and you can find both these in a high quality Omega 3 supplement. Go to your local health store and buy a 1000MG Omega 3 fish oil supplement and take three of these a day, either all at once or spread over the day. Do not buy cod liver oil tablets as they contain a large amount of vitamin A, which may combine with some of the other supplements I am going to ask you to take and cause some rather unpleasant side effects.

It's important that you follow this method to the letter; I understand there is a cost involved with buying high quality supplements, but I promise you it will be significantly less than you are currently spending on alcohol. Do not be tempted to remove any of the recommended steps or supplements from the method (unless you have an underlying medical condition that warrants such a precaution); they are all-effective and work exceptional well together to create our desired outcome of permanent sobriety.

In some recent research, two dozen mice were deliberately given alcohol until they became dependent upon it. From this point on they were allowed to have as much or as little alcohol as they wanted, and their consumption was monitored. Twelve of the mice were removed from the testing area and fed high strength

Omega 3 before being placed back into the test. Despite alcohol being freely available, the twelve mice treated with Omega 3 consumed significantly less alcohol than the untreated animals. Omega 3 is so effective because EPA actually repairs parts of the brain damaged by alcohol. It balances your moods and emotions, plus it's very good for your heart too. DHA is used directly as a material to rebuild brain tissue damaged by the years of napalm you have fired into your brain.

Next, we are going to work on your production of important 'feel good' neuro chemicals. To create healthy amounts of serotonin, melatonin and dopamine, your body and brain need the raw materials that come directly from external sources (they cannot be created independently). Normally you would get enough of these elements from your food (if you were eating a healthy and balanced diet), but we are starting with a handicap, effectively we are trying to start a car with a flat battery on a cold morning. So when you are in the health food store buying your Omega 3, I want you to also buy a good quality multivitamin, it absolutely must contain a decent level of vitamin C, magnesium and zinc. Virtually all high street multivitamins will contain vitamin C, but only the comprehensive A to Z brands will contain the full range of elements. Additionally I would advise you to further increase your intake of vitamin C by eating significantly more citrus fruits, or by adding another supplement of ascorbic acid.

The multivitamin is like a broadsword covering most of your needs up to somewhere near the RDA amount. However, as problem drinkers we are not your average human beings, we need some of the vitamins and minerals in significantly higher dosages than the standard individual. So please also add to your health store shopping basket a once a day B vitamin complex.

All the supplements we have talked about so far are designed to repair the damage done by years of alcohol abuse and ensure the important parts of our brain have the tools they need to work to peak efficiency. The final piece of the supplement jigsaw comes with the amino acid needed to create Serotonin. If you are deficient in this neuro transmitter you can't help but feel depressed. As a problem drinker you are highly likely to be low on this vital chemical.

If you have been consuming an unhealthy amount of alcohol (not that there is a healthy amount) for a significant period of time your brain and body will have already adapted to the new (unhealthy) reality you have created. It's this power of human adaptability that is often underestimated and provides a convenient smoke screen to the problem that lies hidden beneath. If people dropped down dead after a week of heavy drinking do you think the current worldwide epidemic of alcoholism would exist?

There is a famous story of an elderly man who had given a pint of blood once a month for nearly forty years of his life. Eventually the time came where the blood bank advised him that his blood was no longer suitable for donation and while they were very grateful for his years of generosity they could no longer use his blood for medical purposes. The gentleman stopped making his monthly trip to the donation center and it wasn't long before he started to feel very ill. He repeatedly visited his GP complaining of vague symptoms of unease and generally feeling uncomfortable. It took quite sometime before they were able to establish that he simply had too much blood in his system. His body had adapted to losing at least a pint of blood every month without fail. He had become conditioned to producing blood at a rate to compensate and only when the situation changed the adaptation became noticeable.

You have adapted to poison being present in your system and when you stop drinking you may become aware of this adaptation for the first time. This feeling of unease is not caused by the loss of alcohol but rather it is a clear indication of what you body has had to do in order to keep you alive in such a polluted lifestyle. When you quit the booze your brain chemistry will once again be out of balance for a while until it readapts to life as it is supposed to be lived. The method is all about taking the struggle and pain out of giving up drinking so its important that we take some supplements to ensure we don't have to deal with a low mental state during the kick period.

The production of Serotonin is a two-part process that begins in the gut and is completed in the brain. This is a crucial component of my stop drinking method, and can only be created by consuming an amino acid called tryptophan, which is found in turkey, soy beans, tuna, halibut and other fish. The easiest way for us to get the correct amount of tryptophan is to take a supplement called 5-HTP, which stands for 5-Hydroxytryptophan. You need to take two 50MG capsules about 30 minutes before bed with a small sugary drink. This could be a mug of hot chocolate or even just a piece of chocolate if you prefer.

The reason for this specific 5-HTP ritual is this amino acid is transported to the brain by insulin, which is created by the pancreas as a reaction to consuming sugar. If there is plenty of insulin rushing around your system, the 5-HTP will reach its target quicker and more effectively (of course if you are diabetic you should skip this step). We take this supplement last thing at night because the brain converts serotonin into melatonin, which calms our mind and prepares us for the sleep cycle. So, a pleasant side effect of more Serotonin 'happy chemicals' is a better sleep pattern. After a fairly short period of time you should notice that you find it easier to get to sleep and feel more rested when you awake in the morning.

Because of the potential for side effects and interactions with medications, you should take dietary supplements only under the supervision of your health care provider.

Tryptophan use has been associated with the development of serious conditions, such as liver and brain toxicity, and with eosinophilic myalgia syndrome (EMS), a potentially fatal disorder that affects the skin, blood, muscles, and organs (see "Overview" section). Such reports prompted the FDA to ban the sale of all tryptophan supplements in 1989. As with tryptophan, EMS has been reported in 10 people taking 5-HTP.

Side effects of 5-HTP are generally mild and may include nausea, heartburn, gas, feelings of fullness, and rumbling sensations in some people. At high doses, it is possible that serotonin syndrome, a dangerous condition caused by too much serotonin in the body, could develop. Always talk to your health care provider before taking higher-than-recommended doses.

People with high blood pressure or diabetes should talk to their doctor before taking 5-HTP.

If you take antidepressants, you should not take 5-HTP.

People with liver disease, pregnant women, and women who are breastfeeding should not take 5-HTP.

If you are currently being treated with any of the following medications, you should not use 5-HTP without first talking to your health care provider.

Antidepressants -- People who are taking antidepressant medications should not take 5-HTP without their health care provider's supervision. These medications could combine with 5-HTP to cause serotonin syndrome, a dangerous condition involving mental changes, hot flashes, rapidly fluctuating blood pressure and heart rate, and possibly coma. Some antidepressant medications that can interact with 5-HTP include:

- SSRIs: Citalopram (Celexa), escitalopram (Lexapro), fluvoxamine (Luvox), paroxetine (Paxil), fluoxetine (Prozac), sertraline (Zoloft)
- Tricyclics: Amitriptyline (Elavil), nortryptyline (Pamelor), imipramine (Tofranil)
- Monoamine oxidase inhibitors (MAOIs): Phenelzine, (Nardil), tranylcypromine (Parnate)
- Nefazodone (Serzone)

Carbidopa -- Taking 5-HTP with carbidopa, a medication used to treat Parkinson's disease, may cause a scleroderma-like illness. Scleroderma is a condition where the skin becomes hard, thick, and inflamed.

Tramadol (Ultram) -- Tramadol, used for pain relief and sometimes prescribed for people with fibromyalgia, may raise serotonin levels too much if taken with 5-HTP.

Serotonin syndrome has been reported in some people taking the two together.

Dextromethorphan (Robitussin DM, and others) -- Taking 5-HTP with dextromethorphan, found in cough syrups, may cause serotonin levels to increase to dangerous levels, a condition called serotonin syndrome.

Meperidine (Demerol) -- Taking 5-HTP with Demerol may cause serotonin levels to increase to dangerous levels, a condition called serotonin syndrome.

Triptans (used to treat migraines) -- 5-HTP can increase the risk of side effects, including serotonin syndrome, when taken with these medications:

- Naratriptan (Amerge)
- Rizatriptan (Maxalt)
- Sumatriptan (Imitrex)
- Zolmitriptan (Zomig)

You may also hear stories that 5-HTP causes heart valve damage in laboratory mice. This is slightly erroneous information and there are some rather tenuous assumptions being made to reach that particular theory. While it is true that injected serotonin does create a small risk of heart valve disease in scientific animals, the same does not appear to apply to orally ingested serotonin.

However, that said and with all supplements, if you have any reason to be concerned (such as a pre-existing heart condition), you are advised to ask your doctors advice before starting on any supplement.

B Vitamins

Vitamin B12 is a water-soluble vitamin that keeps your nerves and red blood cells healthy. It is responsible for the smooth functioning of several critical body processes.

It is possible for the body to develop a vitamin B12 deficiency. This deficiency is usually reported with symptoms of fatigue. As you can imagine the last thing you need when trying to lose weight is a lack of energy.

Strict vegetarians, heavy drinkers and smokers, pregnant and breast-feeding women, and the elderly usually require vitamin B12 supplements. Sometimes our body, mainly our digestive system, is not able to absorb this vitamin well. This can happen when a person has pernicious anemia, celiac disease, Crohn's disease, bacteria growth in the small intestine, or a parasite.

A deficiency in vitamin B12 can result in a host of illnesses like anemia, fatigue, weakness, constipation, loss of appetite, weight loss, depression, poor memory, soreness of the mouth, asthma, vision problems, and a low sperm count.

The top 5 health benefits of vitamin B 12 are:

• It is needed to convert carbohydrates into glucose in the body, thus leading to energy production and a decrease in fatigue and lethargy in the body.
• B12 helps in healthy regulation of the nervous system, reducing depression, stress, and brain shrinkage.

• It helps maintain a healthy digestive system. Vitamin B12 also protects against heart disease by curbing and improving unhealthy cholesterol levels, protecting against stroke, and high blood pressure.

• B12 is essential for healthy skin, hair, and nails. It helps in cell reproduction and constant renewal of the skin.

• Vitamin B 12 helps protect against cancers including breast, colon, lung, and prostrate cancer.

Yet again your daily multivitamin is not going to cut it. If you are anything like me (back when I was a drinker) you may have been abusing your body for a long time with alcohol. I take an additional B Vitamin complex on top of my multivitamin and having read the possible results of being deficient in this area I am sure you can see why it is an important addition to your own daily routine.

Vitamin D

There is a pandemic of Vitamin D deficiency that is causing ill health, lethargy and weight gain around the world. The problem has been created by our modern lifestyle choices, increased alcohol consumption, several key incorrect assumptions and the cutthroat dollars and cents mentality behind our medical research techniques.

A deficiency in Vitamin D has been linked to diseases from Dementia, Chron's and Cancer to the repeated appearance of the common cold and flu.

I have witnessed the effects of Vitamin D deficiency first hand. A few years ago my daughter Aoife started to complain about pain in her bones and skin. She also started to get random and volatile swings in mood and behavior. As she was just entering that difficult phase of life that involves leaving childhood behind and becoming a teenager, as such we initially put these symptoms down to growing pains and the sort of general teenage moodiness all kids go through.

However, the symptoms slowly got worse and worse until she was taking an unhealthy amount of pain relief just to get through each day. The doctors initially assumed an anti-immune disorder was most likely, as her mother had already been diagnosed Lupus (SLE). Thankfully the blood test was negative for the SLE markers and all the other serious conditions they checked her for.

Coincidently this was around the time I was starting to research Vitamin D and Magnesium and it struck me that a lot of the symptoms I was reading about sounded very similar to what Aoife was complaining about. I suggested to the doctor that we test for these two elements. The magnesium test came back first and it showed no problem but a few days later we got a telephone call to say Aoife was severely Vitamin D deficient and they were going to prescribe a daily supplement.

As most people know the best source of Vitamin D are the UV rays of the sun. These rays stimulate a process in the skin that creates an inactive form of the vitamin. The liver then converts this inert substance into a powerful and vital element that is important to health and longevity. The problem is, over the last century our lifestyles have changed faster and more profoundly than in any period before. Human beings in the past have been predominately outdoor, manual workers until relatively recently in our evolution.

Agricultural and industrial work dominated until the information age came along. We no longer work the fields but rather tend to sit in front of a computer monitor all day long before going home to then sit in front of a bigger screen until bedtime. Children no longer play games in the streets and climb trees for fun. You are much more likely to see them sitting in front of a games console killing Zombies with an AK47 (unaware of the irony that they look a bit like zombies themselves).

False Assumption One:
We can get all the Vitamin D we need from a few minutes sunshine each day.

This is not true as the assumption is too broad. That theory might be perfectly adequate when applied to fair skinned people living near or on the equator of the earth. However, several factors will mean that it is an ineffective solution to virtually all other people.

• The darker your skin the less well you create Vitamin D.
• The strength of the UV rays dramatically decreases the further north of the equator you go.
• We have slowly become terrified of the sun and now routinely apply sunscreen to ourselves and our children as part of our daily routine.
• A sunscreen with a sun protection factor of 8+ will block over 96% of the UV rays needed by your skin to produce vitamin D.

Not only are we most employed on an indoor basis but also many people now choose to eat their lunch in front of their workstation. The concept of a lunch hour has been eroded by career ambitions and the financial climate.

The reality is that our lifestyles have slowly changed and moved us out of the sunlight. It will be several hundred thousand years before evolution catches up. So you can either wait or start taking a supplement – your choice!

False Assumption Two:

Vitamin D is just another vitamin and no more important that any of the others.

Our blasé approach to supplements causes a problem here because it fails to give Vitamin D the spotlight it deserves. Actually the problem is more to do with the label, Vitamin D is not actually a vitamin but rather it is an essential hormone.

A hormone is a substance that is produced in one part of the body but has a wide-ranging effect on various other important parts of the body such as the brain, heart and other vital organs.

Vitamin D is so much more than a vitamin, it is as essential to good health as sleep, food and exercise.

False Assumption Three:

If Vitamin D was the solution to all the problems
mentioned then surely my doctor would test for it and
recommend it as an effective treatment.
The reality is that you are most likely to have never been
tested for Vitamin D deficiency and here is the reason
why:

Vitamin D fails to make it onto the medical training
agenda and into doctor's surgeries due to the dollars and
cents mentality of our medical research. Pharmaceutical
companies do not strive for a cure for cancer because
they are lovely caring people with a determination to see
us all live a long and healthy life but rather the truth is;
developing and then monopolizing a cure for a serious
disease or illness means massive profits for their
shareholders. Vitamin D is inexpensive and freely

available around the world, over the counter and without prescription and therefore it is worthless to the medical research companies out to invent the next miracle cure. Sadly most of the information fed into our doctors and medical training facilities still comes directly from the major pharmaceutical companies.

Combine this selective hearing of the medical community with the out of date information still being peddled by governments who are still quoting dosage information long since out of date and you have Vitamin D left sitting on the shelf.

Vitamin D and Weight Loss:

On top of all the other health benefits of Vitamin D there is an interesting side effect that is weight reduction (or perhaps a better phrase would be weight correction). I am not suggesting taking a D supplement for this reason alone but it is a pleasant added bonus to what I consider to be a true miracle addition to any diet.

There are a lot of empty calories in alcohol and I am sure my unhealthy consumption of a daily bottle of wine added to the extra 60lbs of fat I was also carrying around. So for many people hooked on booze and looking to stop there is an additional bonus in the potential weight loss they will see as a result of their actions. There have been several studies that have linked vitamin D to weight loss. Vitamin D has been shown to be very effective in increasing the amount of body fat loss while increasing your energy levels at the same time. By increasing your energy levels, the body can overcome chronic fatigue and lethargic moods.

One of the latest research studies conducted by the University of Minnesota discovered that people with weight problems would have more success in losing weight if their vitamin D levels are increased to a higher level. The lead researcher, Dr. Shalamar Sibley, found solid evidence that out of 38 obese men and women, the people that had a higher vitamin D level were able to lose more weight than those who had a lower level of vitamin D.

So how much do you take?

Again I will remind you that I am not a doctor and you must do your own research before taking any of the supplements. All I can do here is tell you what I personally take and explain why I do so.

The 'out of date' recommended daily allowance for Vitamin D, and what you will most likely see quoted on the side of your multivitamin bottle is 200 iu per day. When I discovered what the leading experts in this field are now recommending I was blown away by just how inaccurate the government official RDA is.

Vitamin D can be taken monthly, weekly or daily. Personally I just add it as part of my morning routine, that way I can keep a close eye on what I am doing and how it is effecting me. I recommend adding a vitamin D supplement to your diet at an amount of 20 iu per pound of body weight. For example, I weigh in at 192 lbs and so I take 3900 iu per day. You can expect to see noticeable improvements and health, mobility and weight between two weeks and three months after starting supplementation.

Obviously you will need to recalculate you dosage on a regular basis as your body weight starts to fall.

If you are interesting in reading more about the Vitamin D pandemic and why this hormone is so vital and yet so over looked then please read:

The Vitamin D Cure by James Dowd
The Power of Vitamin D by Sarfraz Zaidi

Other Essential Supplements

Vitamin K2
There is a delicate balance between Vitamin D and K2. It is vital that if you are supplementing your diet with high strength Vitamin D that you also take a daily Vitamin K2 tablet.

Magnesium

Another vital element that goes hand in hand with your Vitamin D supplementation is the mineral magnesium.

Magnesium is an essential mineral for staying healthy and is required for more than 300 biochemical reactions in the body. Multiple health benefits of magnesium include transmission of nerve impulses, body temperature regulation, detoxification, energy production, and the formation of healthy bones and teeth.

Health specialists have always emphasized the importance of including adequate amounts of vitamins and minerals in our daily diet. Zinc, calcium, and magnesium are three of the most important minerals essential for good health. Magnesium aids in the absorption of calcium by the body, while zinc actively supports the body's immune system.

Women of all ages benefit immensely from the intake of magnesium. Besides keeping osteoporosis at bay, magnesium health benefits in women include relief from symptoms of menopause and premenstrual syndrome (PMS). It also minimizes the risk of premature labor.

The other crucial health benefits of magnesium include protein synthesis, relief from bronchospasm (constricted airways) in the lungs, and improvement of parathyroid function. It boosts the bio-availability of vitamin B6 and cholesterol, improves muscle functioning, and prevents osteoporosis, insomnia, constipation, heart attacks, hypertension, migraines, kidney stones, and gallstones.

Good dietary sources of magnesium include nuts (especially almonds), whole grains, wheat germ, fish, and green leafy vegetables. As with most nutrients, daily needs for magnesium cannot be met from food alone which is why magnesium dietary supplements are recommended as well.

The top five health benefits of magnesium are:

1. Magnesium may reverse osteoporosis

Multiple research studies conducted have suggested that calcium supplemented with magnesium improves bone mineral density. Magnesium deficiency alters calcium metabolism and the hormones that regulate calcium, resulting in osteoporosis. Intake of recommended levels of magnesium is important because it averts osteoporosis.

2. Magnesium prevents cardiovascular diseases

One of the most important benefits of magnesium is that it is associated with lowering the risk of coronary heart diseases. Dietary surveys have suggested that sufficient magnesium intake may reduce the chance of having a stroke. Magnesium deficiency increases the risk of abnormal heart rhythms, which increases the risk of complications after a heart attack. Therefore, consuming recommended amounts of magnesium dietary supplements may be beneficial to the cardiovascular system.

3. Magnesium regulates high blood pressure

Magnesium plays a key role in regulating blood pressure naturally. Magnesium supplements and a diet including plenty of fruits and vegetables, which are good sources of potassium and magnesium, are consistently associated with lowering blood pressure.

4. Magnesium treats diabetes

Studies show that individuals with a magnesium deficiency have a risk of developing type-2 diabetes and severe diabetic retinopathy. Magnesium aids in carbohydrate metabolism and influences the release and activity of insulin, thereby controlling blood glucose levels. It has been proven that for every 100 milligrams of increase in magnesium daily intake, there was a 15 percent decrease in the risk of developing type-2 diabetes.

5. Magnesium treats migraines, insomnia, & depression

The numerous magnesium health benefits also include the treatment of migraines, insomnia, and symptoms of depression. Magnesium is also known to cure severe forms of psychiatric dysfunctions including panic attacks, stress, anxiety, and undue agitations. Magnesium supplements considerably reduce the severity of such attacks and may also help in reducing the rate of recurrence.

Chapter Eleven
Controlling the ego

It does appear to the casual reader that you are now into what could be described as 'the cure' section of the book. In these shorter chapters I am giving you specific things to do, that I know will help you stop drinking. However, if you have skipped forward to this point you will miss the whole point of the book. My method is a six-step programme, and the 'cure' is delivered through every chapter and not just the final four.

At this point I don't want you to be worried that so far I appear to have only given you a list of vitamins to buy from the heath food store. You may be worried that it sounds too easy and could be asking the question 'there must be more to it than popping a few pills'?

Don't worry, because there is, and indeed after reading this book if the only thing you did was to go out and buy the supplements I mentioned in chapter ten, I am almost certain you would not stop drinking as a result.

If you only follow through on half the steps in this book then there is only a very slim chance you will give up the booze. So finely balanced is the process that even if you successfully complete five of the six steps, I still wouldn't express my total confidence in you to achieve the sober outcome you desire. This method works for so many people because the whole is far greater than the sum of its parts. It's the combination of multiple levels of theory that combine to cause a paradigm shift significant enough to change your thinking and subconscious programming.

Whether you believe in a step or not, please do not remove it from the method. Each one of the six steps work hand in hard with the next to create the desired outcome. The first step you actually achieved long before you even picked this book up; the decision that you are sick and tired or feeling sick and tired. An awareness that alcohol is starting to create more problems than it solves. This is a beautiful stage to get to, because at this point you stop being a part of the 80% who refuse to admit that they have a problem and you move into an elite bunch of people who are ready to take action.

Step two was what I explained to you over the first nine chapters of this book. To completely claim step two has been successfully completed you should by this point agree with me that alcohol is not an inoffensive social pleasantry, but a deviously packaged and promoted addictive drug. The lies that you previously believed should now be clear to see for what they really are, and you cannot logically see any benefit to the further consumption of alcohol. If this is not the case and you still believe that if you stop drinking you will be denying yourself something special, then this method and any other method you care to try will fail.

It is virtually impossible to give up something that you still believe is a positive attribute in your life. This is exactly why 95% of alcoholics that join AA end up relapsing. If you still want to drink because you believe it tastes good, makes you more confident, helps you relax or any of the other lies, then do yourself a favor;

- [ ] Turn back to page one and start again – many need to read this book numerous times before the penny drops.

- [ ] Start researching the true effects of alcohol for yourself and get piles of evidence to demonstrate the reality of this drug.

- [ ] Take a look at my other books on the subject, including 'The Alcohol Illusion' which clearly shows you how deception alcohol can be.

Unless you can honestly say that you feel differently about alcohol now there is no point buying the vitamins and supplements mentioned in step three. There is no advantage in moving onto step four, if the first and second parts of the method are not 100% nailed on.

If you are still reading, congratulations! That means you have checked off step one and two and now have a list in your hand ready to take to the health food store that says:

- Broad spectrum 'once a day' multivitamin
- B Vitamin Complex
- Omega 3 1000MG capsules
- 50MG 5-HTP supplement *
- Vitamin C tablets.
- Vitamin D tablets 2500 IU

> *If you are taking any other prescription medication please check with your doctor before taking 5-HTP.

You are now ready for step four. This section addresses one of the most important keys to stopping drinking – the egoic tendency to predict failure.

I need you to become aware of your conscious mind's attempts to seize control. It happens so often that this step can appear to be quite a challenge. Sometimes it appears so monumental a task that you are not quite sure where to start.

Let me give you a list of examples of your ego attempting a hijack you:

• You try a dress on and it feels a bit tight, you start to feel bad because it used to fit perfectly. This is your ego pulling the past into the future.

• Your boss criticizes your work and you start to think about all thing things that he gets wrong. How dare he talk to you like that, does he not know how much time you spent on that project etc. This is an attack on your ego and your ego is responding.

• You are driving and someone cuts you up and beeps their horn at you, instantly you beep back, outraged that they are blaming you for their mistake! You consider for a brief moment what you should do next. This is an attack on your ego and your ego is responding.

• You are going to a party later and you find yourself worrying about how you will cope without a drink. This is your ego predicting failure.

All thoughts of the past and future must be generated by the ego / conscious because from the subconscious mind's point of view they don't exist and so can't be considered. These thoughts are not universally negative, but they are highly unlikely to be positive. For example... Even if you get excited thinking about seeing your children or partner later, there is always a negative connotation attached to the anticipation

e.g. 'I can't wait to get home and play with my children, I wish it was 5pm already'.

Even though you might consider this to be a positive thought process, the ego is still suggesting that happiness lies in a different time and not in the precise moment you are currently experiencing.

231

You don't need to use willpower to try to stop this happening; all I am asking you to do is be aware of it happening. Laugh at it when you spot it, welcome it back as an old friend. It is actually your awareness of it happening that causes it to lose power. Once you start realizing that your ego and you are not the same thing, amazing and beautiful things start to appear in your life.

I am acutely aware it may sound far too simple and perhaps even too good to be true. But even that is just a conscious prediction of failure generated by your ego.

Don't take my word for it, take a leap of faith and for the next 21 days assume it's true... just watch the difference!

The egoic need to predict the future is a particular problem to someone trying to quit drinking alcohol because it is a powerful motivator of human behavior and will provide quite compelling arguments that your life will be less enjoyable without booze. The ego hates any form of change that comes from an external force; it simply doesn't like anything that implies that it is not in full control of your life.

Here are some of the common false predictions generated by the ego in response to stopping drinking:

- *Going to social occasions will no longer be any fun*
- *Vacations will be less pleasurable in the sober future*
- *You will have no way of relaxing after a stressful day*
- *There will be no way to celebrate in the future*
- *You will struggle to get to sleep after you stop drinking*

If any of those thoughts have entered your mind as you consider taking the next step on your journey to a dry life I would like you to recognize that they are nothing but the senile ramblings of your ego attempting to do something it is completely incapable of doing; predicting the future. When you catch yourself thinking about drinking, consider whether any part of the thought is coming from a memory of the past or a predication of the future and recognize at this point that it is only the ego in a panic about what you are doing. Pull yourself back into the moment that we call the 'now'.

Henrik Edburg puts it well when he says there are lots of advantages to living in the moment including:

♣ Clarity. When you are in the moment you have a much better focus and things flow naturally out of you. This is very useful in conversations, at work, while writing or even while doing fun stuff such as playing golf.

♣ Calmness. You feel centered, relaxed and whatever you do you do more easily. Since you are not projecting into a possible future or reflecting on previous experiences there is very little fear holding you back.

♣ Positivity. Since there is little fear, there are few negative emotions when you are in the present. Instead you move around on positive part of the emotional scale.

How do you actually return to the present moment?

Here are 7 ways. But before we get to them I'd just like to add that this is a skill. You will slip back into involuntarily thinking about the future/past. But the more time and effort you spend connecting with the moment the easier it gets reconnecting with it and staying there longer.

1. Focus on what's right in front of you.

Or around you. Or on you. Use your senses. Just look at what's right in front of you right now. Listen to the sounds around you. Feel the fabric of your clothes and focus on how they feel.

2. Focus on your breathing.

Take a couple of dozen belly breaths and just focus your mind on your inhaling and exhaling. This will align you with the present moment once again.

3. Focus on your inner body.

This is a bit similar to focusing on your breathing. In both examples you focus on what's inside you rather than the outside. What is the inner body? Well, I guess you could say it is energy inside of your body. How your body feels from the inside.

A practical way to do this is just to focus on your hand. To just put your focus there and feel how the hand feels to you and how the energy is flowing through it.

4. Pick up the vibe from present people.

If you know someone that is more present than most people then you can pick his/her vibe of presence (just like you can pick up positivity or enthusiasm from people).

If you don't know someone like that I recommend listening to audiobooks by Eckhart Tolle, Brian Tracy, Anthony Robbins, Zig Ziglar or any of the other respected personal development authors out there.

5. Surrender to the emotion that is already there.

It's easy to get stuck in a loop of old memories. You may want to move away from them but there is a feeling there that brings them back over and over. So you need to decrease the power that feeling has over you. And you don't do it by fighting it. You do it by surrendering to it. The feeling is a loop within your mind that you are feeding with more energy by resisting it. When you accept the feeling then you stop feeding it and it vanishes.

Here's how you do it:

Say yes to the feeling.

Surrender and let it in. Observe the feeling in your mind and body without labeling or judging it. If you let it in – for me the feeling then often seems to physically locate itself to the middle of my chest – and just observe it for maybe a minute or two the feeling just vanishes.

6. See things as for the first time.

This one pretty similar to the first way. But it can be useful when you have a hard time just observing your surroundings.

That's when you can look at things as for the first time. Imagine it like that, take that role. Like someone who has never experienced this before. Like a child or someone who has never been here before.

Note: These last two ways are certainly not the best ways to reconnect with the moment and I'm not really recommending them. They aren't that healthy (especially in the long run). But they work to some degree. It's up to you if you want to try them.

7. A pinch or a punch!

Try punching your leg, or pinching your arm. Or have someone else do it. And focus on that sensation to quickly bring yourself back to the moment.

Don't go crazy; I am not trying to turn you into a masochist or anything. Just give yourself a little nip and then take a few seconds to experience the feeling. It is purely a distraction that pulls you away from the past or future and allows you to center once again in the present moment.

Chapter Twelve
Dealing with the kick

For most people, once they no longer see alcohol as a benefit, they simply don't want to drink anymore, and so they don't. For others it takes a little time for the information to be absorbed and to stick. A seed of change has been planted and over the next few weeks you will observe a lot more of the negative effects of alcohol than you ever noticed before. You will see friends at parties slurring their words and believing they are truly master orators holding court. You will be surprised that they cannot see that they are anesthetized buffoons talking 100% proof gibberish.

You will notice the sexualisation of alcohol by the advertising industry. Of course typically, the term sex really refers to beautiful women (and increasingly, handsome men) that are used to lure in a potential drinker despite a tenuous a non-existent link to the brand being advertised.

You will see television commercials for alcohol and see just how devious they are. Watch them with a critical eye and see how they use sex to hook us in to their killer product.

It's been said that as human beings, we have a lizard or reptilian brain that responds to certain primal urges. Food is one. Sex and reproduction is definitely another. This underlying, pre-programmed disposition to respond to sexual imagery is so strong, it has been used for over 100 years in advertising. And the industry, while abusing it more and more, would be foolish to ignore the draw of sexual and erotic messaging.

Back in 1885, W.Duke and Sons, a manufacturer of facial soap, included trading cards in the soap's packaging that included erotic images of the day's most popular female stars. The link between soap and sex is slim at best, but the link between alcohol and sex is equally as tenuous and that works just as well.

Does Sex Actually Sell?

Yes, sex sells. It's a fact. Popular men's magazines like Maxim and FHM have experimented often with their covers. Overwhelmingly, when a sexy, semi-naked woman appears on the cover, it outperforms an image of a male star, even if that star is someone men want to read about.

When ads are more sexually provocative, men in particular are irresistibly drawn to them. It's simple genetics. Men respond to sexual images. And if your ad creates a sexual situation, it will get the desired response.

When you consider the science and theory behind sexual advertising you can see how devious and dishonest it is as a way to encourage people to consume an addictive drug. Using sexual images to tug on genetic responses from customers is a pretty underhand way to encourage use of a product that is for all intents and purposes a poison. The only reasonable excuse for using sex to promote alcohol would be that it did what it claimed to do. If when you drank a specific brand of booze you looked physically more attractive then fair enough. However, when you live a life free of this attractively packaged poison you will notice how ugly and repulsive people under the effect of this drug actually become.

Here's a challenge we make in the 'Alcohol Lied to Me' members website... After you have been alcohol free for a couple of months, the first time you kiss or make out with someone who has been drinking report back to the site and anonymously describe the experience. To date nobody has told us that kissing a drunk person was a more pleasurable experience - indeed often words such as 'stale', 'tainted' and 'disgusting' get used in the description.

Alcohol advertising tries to create positives from the vast array of negatives generated by this drug. The industry knows that alcohol creates a withdrawal symptom that feels similar to stress and so they make commercials that portray alcohol as a form of relaxation.

When a colleague tells you they can't wait to get home, open a bottle of wine and relax, you will see that statement for what it really is. You now know this ritual has nothing to do with relaxation, but rather it is a vocalization of the symptoms of an alcohol kick which by the end of the working day is approaching peak intensity.

Observe these lies being told all around you by your friends, family and colleagues, but do not feel the urge to point out your observations to anyone. Shining a light on things that people have deliberately placed in the dark is a direct attack on someone's ego, and you can expect nothing but a hostile defense in reply.

For two weeks, providing you don't drink again, your alcohol withdrawal symptoms will get weaker every day. Over that period and for a few weeks after, the supplements you are now taking will slowly begin to have a positive effect. They do not work overnight and they work differently for everyone. Some people report a massive improvement within a week, others only notice the impact after a month, and a lot of people are not aware of anything happening until they stop taking them and realize what the supplements were contributing.

If during this period (or at anytime) you get the urge to drink, and you can't pull yourself into the now. When the cravings are so strong that you feel like there is nothing you can do to stop yourself from pouring a drink, I want you to use a technique called Thought Field Therapy or TFT. Again, this is a principle that appears to be so simple you can't imagine it providing any tangible benefit.

TFT is an acupuncture technique based on the tapping on specific meridian points in the upper body. A renowned Clinical Psychologist called Roger Callahan discovered the principle of TFT in 1980 when he theorized that all negative thought patterns are actually similar to computer programs that are universally shared by all humans. This is why fear feels the same to me as it does to you, we both run exactly the same programme and so we experience the same physical and mental symptoms of fear accordingly. His system demonstrates that by using unique pressure points in the body we can literally turn off the programme. It's like a CTRL-ALT-DEL option for negative emotions, anxiety, and most importantly in our case, cravings.

Next time you need to turn off your cravings for a drink, simply find a quite room, anywhere will do. Using your index and middle finger gently start tapping on your cheek bone, directly under the corner of your eye. Tap between ten and twenty times before repeating the process just above your eyebrow. Keep alternating the meridian point and before each change ask yourself honestly how much you need a drink.

With each series of tapping, give the craving a score out of ten. You may start around the nine or ten level of 'need', but you should find that the number slowly reduces with each sequence. Slowly you will find that your desperation moves from 'must have' to 'like to have' before reaching your goal point of 'I can take it or leave it'.

This step is easily dismissed as new age mumbo jumbo, but I don't need you to take my word for it, a quick Google search for evidence of Thought Field Therapy success will show you how successful this technique has been for thousands, if not hundreds of thousands, of other people just like you. There are also plenty of videos showing you how to use this technique at my website.

During the kick you may experience a few strange sensations. It is highly likely you will dream about drinking alcohol, this is not because you want to drink, but rather a reflection of what is top of your priority list at the moment. Obviously you are addressing alcohol as a problem in your life, and so your dreams are built around your current focus. This is why after watching a movie you can sometimes dream a similar plotline to what you have just seen, but with yourself playing the role of the protagonist.

When I stopped drinking I would often wake in the morning feeling absolutely convinced I had been drinking heavily the night before, sometimes the dreams were so vivid I would check the garbage for alcohol bottles. Don't be afraid or question the significance of these dreams, as with everything else you observe, simply smile and acknowledge them. These dreams are a good sign, they are evidence that you are going through exactly the same series of events that I did, and the end result of that is a complete repulsion to the thought of drinking another alcoholic drink.

Another slightly strange thing to expect is dealing with a slight sense of loss when in situations where you would have previously consumed alcohol.

Before I moved to Cyprus we used to take regular family vacations on the island. Our vacations usually involved a lot of swimming, reading, sunbathing, eating and of course drinking. There is that unwritten rule that when you are on holiday you can drink anytime of the day. In the past I would have had my first alcoholic drink by the pool at around 10am and slowly kept topping up until bedtime.

The first time we took a vacation after I had quit drinking if felt unusual and a little uncomfortable to be pouring out a soda where I would normally have grabbed a cold beer from the refrigerator. My ex-wife was still drinking at this point, and that intensified the sensations somewhat. I wasn't jealous of my wife and her glass of wine, I absolutely did not want to drink, but something felt wrong.

Later that night we walked into the seafront bar we would go to most evenings. The owner is a Greek Cypriot called Andreas, and he had always made us feel like old friends returning home. He would play jokes with the kids (including pretending to pour vodka into their lemonade, which made them feel all grown up just like mum and dad).

This particular evening, as we walked into the bar he noticed us immediately. He rushed out from behind his bar to greet us warmly before ushering us to a table overlooking the Mediterranean. We exchanged small talk for a few moments before he waved at the barmaid still working behind the bar. A few moments later she came over to join us with a tray of drinks.

Andreas proudly demonstrated his amazing memory again. Despite not having seen us for nearly a year he placed our usual order of drinks on the table in front of us. A cold glass of wine in front of Denise...

"White for Mrs Beck" he said in a soft Greek accent.

Next he reached for two almost fluorescent drinks, tall glasses with a concoction of liquids. The drinks were green at the top, orange most of the way down before turning bright red at the bottom.

"Special cocktails for the children, one Vodka and one Bacardi'", he said with a wink at the grown ups.

My two children giggled at the suggestion, they knew there was nothing in those glasses but fruit juice and syrup, but they liked the idea that someone might overhear the announcement. It made them feel 'part of the grown ups gang', such is the social conditioning of the alcohol drug that children feel like they are missing out on something special!

I smiled as Jordan and Aoife slurped enthusiastically at their 'cocktails', and then the smile dropped from my face as a huge frosted glass of Leon (the local beer) was lowered from the tray and presented to me.

"Yammas", Andreas cheered and started to walk away.

A few seconds passed by, and I wondered what to do. I didn't want to insult Andreas by sending back the drink, but I most certainly didn't want to drink it. Then I considered that I had not really put much thought into why we had gone to bar in the first place. What was I going to drink? Would I get bored?

We used to spend the whole evening in there, slowly getting anesthetized together. When nobody was looking I tipped the beer into a plant pot and quickly ordered a soft drink to be sure he wouldn't diligently refill my glass as he normally would.

I admit, in those moments I felt like I had lost something, and it made me feel sad. This feeling was tinged with confusion because I was also very aware that I didn't want the thing I had lost. You too will experience these moments, maybe at a wedding or social gathering where all the drinks are provided free. Someone will push one into your hand and for a moment you will feel sad because you don't want to join in and drink it. In those moments you must remind yourself that the way you feel has nothing to do with the alcohol, it is purely a conditioned response.

A completely unrelated incident that happened in Cyprus helped me get used to the new sober me. The car hire company had messed up our reservation and when we got to the airport collection desk they didn't have any record of our booking. They were very apologetic and eventually found us a car, but it was an automatic and not a manual drive. I had never driven an automatic before and I found not using my left foot or the gear stick very unsettling. For the first few days I drove that car like a complete novice driver, I sat forward in my chair hugging the steering wheel, concentrating intensely on every single maneuver. I felt exceptionally uncomfortable for about three days, and then it became 'automatic', if you will excuse the pun.

When I got back home to the UK and jumped in my manual car, I again felt uncomfortable and clumsy. This is exactly what happens when you are put in situations where in the past you would have drunk. It's not the lack of alcohol that is making you feel bad, it's the slightly uncomfortable sensation of not responding as you are automatically conditioned to do.

If I strapped your right arm to your side and made you live your life for a whole year without using that limb, imagine how strange it would feel using your right hand again after a year. This is how you may feel in circumstances where you would have previously had an alcoholic drink. The more you embed the new reality, the easier it gets; so enjoy each one of those uncomfortable moments and see them as another step on the road to a lifetime of happy sobriety.

Chapter Thirteen
F.S.Q (Frequently Slurred Questions)

Forgive the quirky play on words because this section of 'Alcohol Lied to Me' may serve a very valuable purpose in your mission to escape the cycle of alcohol addiction. Over the years I have had many questions emailed to me from problem drinkers (mostly look for reasons why it would be okay for them to carry on with their drug of choice).

No doubt some of the queries in this ever-expanding section of the book may have popped into your head at some point, so here goes:

Q1. I really want to stop drinking but I work with a pretty tough bunch of guys and if I didn't drink with them I wouldn't hear the end of it. Should I just cut down rather than stop drinking?

A1. I can really empathize with your situation because we live in a bizarre world where heavy drinking has somehow become associated with being a 'real man'. Back when I was a drinker I had quite a reputation for being able to 'hold my drink'. As we now know this tolerance for alcohol should be seen as the first symptom of a serious problem with an addictive drug and not the positive trait that social males so often dictate that it is. I stopped drinking in the winter, November actually. In the past I would have postponed this attempt to January because you can't go through a Christmas season without drinking can you (yet another funny lie we have been force fed).

When I woke up and realized that it is the rest of the world that is wrong about booze and not me I just decided I didn't want to drink it anymore, so the month had no relevance to me.

However, as easy as I found it to no longer drink I still had to attend the traditional Christmas party with all my old drinking buddies.

The evening started in a local pub and my friend Roy walked up to the bar and ordered himself a pint of strong imported beer, he turned to me and said 'same?'. I shook my head and instead asked for a diet coke. A few moment of time passed without further comment and then it began:

"A coke, I am not ordering you a coke. Have a beer and man up", Roy exclaimed, absolutely disgusted at the very suggestion.

"It's ok Roy I am fine with a coke", I replied

"What's wrong with you man, have you turned gay or something", Roy came back.

Perhaps the most ridiculous statement I have ever heard!

I am not sure of the logic behind assuming a decision to no longer voluntarily ingest a toxic chemical must be the result of a change in sexuality but sadly it's a statement thrown at heterosexual men who regain control of alcohol all over the world. Drinking vast quantities of alcohol does not prove you are a tough, red blooded 'mans man'! It proves you are addicted to a common drug!

These sorts of macho put downs are ridiculous and laughable but how do you deal with them?

You tough it out! Eventually your friends will get used to the new healthier you. The problem as we have already discussed is it's your new high standards highlighting the other person's low standards that causes them pain and their ego will not tolerate it. Obviously the best way for them to remove that nagging pain is to also stop drinking but because the ego hates all form of loss it can't accept that prospect and would much rather you started drinking again as a substitute solution.

These days Roy doesn't even need to ask me what I want to drink; he just goes up to the bar orders himself a pint and a diet coke for me. He might mutter some comical insult as he hands it too me but he has accepted the situation and so will your friends – do not bend to their attempts to persuade you back into the mousetrap.

Q2. I have heard that Milk Thistle protects the liver, can I continue drinking if I take it?

A2. Milk thistle (Silybum marianum) has been used for 2,000 years as an herbal remedy for a variety of ailments, particularly liver, kidney, and gall bladder problems. Several scientific studies suggest that substances in milk thistle (especially a flavonoid called silymarin) protect the liver from toxins, including certain drugs such as acetaminophen (Tylenol), which can cause liver damage in high doses. Silymarin has antioxidant and anti-inflammatory properties, and it may help the liver repair itself by growing new cells.

Although a number of animal studies demonstrate that milk thistle can be helpful in protecting the liver, results in human studies are mixed.

Milk thistle is often suggested as a treatment for alcoholic hepatitis and alcoholic cirrhosis. But scientific studies show inconclusive results. Most studies show milk thistle improves liver function and increases survival in people with cirrhosis or chronic hepatitis. But problems in the design of the studies (such as small numbers of participants and differences in dosing and duration of milk thistle therapy) make it hard to draw any real conclusions.

Whether milk thistle helps or not is a gamble you can choose to take if you want. If you are seriously considering continuing to drink and supplementing your diet with milk thistle then I would suggest you have missed the point of this book. Such an act would imply that there is a benefit to continuing to drink alcohol and this is quite frankly insane!

Alcohol is attractively packaged poison backed by a devious and misleading multi billion dollar marketing campaign. The solution you are suggesting is likely to be as effective as the smokers who believed that if they

didn't inhale deeply they wouldn't be at such a high risk
of developing lung cancer. Any thoughts of ways that you
can carry on drinking are just more evidence that you
need to get this poison out of your system once and for
all.

Q3. How do I avoid drinking at Christmas, Thanksgiving and other social occasions?

A3. Well let me start by asking you how you manage to
avoid injecting heroin at Christmas time?

That might sounds like a silly question but in reality there
are only two differences between alcohol and heroin.
Firstly it is just a case of social acceptability, everyone
drinks at Christmas and so we make the false assumption
that it is therefore harmless. Just because everyone is
doing it does not make it a safe activity, you only have to
go back a few decades and the same twisted logic was
applied to smoking. The social proof of smoking did not
prevent millions of people from dying in agony from lung
cancer.

Alcohol is attractively packaged poison whether one person drinks it or a whole nation consumes it.

The second difference between heroin and booze is to do with the kick. All addictive substances will punish you if you try to stop your interaction with them, this is known as 'the kick'. Class A street drugs such as heroin trap their users so successfully because the punishment from stopping using is so severe that it takes great determination and endurance to suffer the kick.

The pain of a heroin kick is beyond anything you can imagine and addicts must endure days of this agony with the knowledge that the pain would vanish in less than a second if they just took another hit of the drug.

Having said that if you really believe that alcohol has the power to make you feel good then you would not believe the power of heroin. This drug can create the feeling of pure ecstasy, a sensation of pleasure beyond our dreams. So here is the big question... why don't you long for heroin at Christmas and Thanksgiving, it is far superior to alcohol?

The reason we coming back to is you do not see any benefit to taking heroin. You would not see it as an enhancement to your life – your thinking about this drug is perfectly logical and as it should be about such a dangerous poison. The problem is your thinking about (alcohol) is twisted.

If you are thinking about how you can survive your birthday party without a drink this is just a clear marker that your thinking is still distorted. Really you should be thinking about how good it is going to feel to have your first birthday in years that won't result in a horrific hangover.

As far as Christmas is concerned the alcohol has only been added in relatively recent times because it provides a convenient excuse to consume more of our favorite drug. Whether you are religious or not consider whether booze figures anywhere in the traditional story of the birth of Christ? Of course it doesn't, the three wise men did not turn up with a crate of beer, a bottle of vodka and some coffee liqueur. These are the trappings of a society trapped in their relationship with an addictive drug. Look to the east with other similar festivals such as the Hindu celebration of light Diwali. Five days of festivities, full of fun, laughter, dancing and merriment... any yet not a single drop of alcohol will cross anyone's lips!

If people tell you that you can't have a good Christmas without a drink, what they are actually saying to you is: "I can't cope without alcohol, not even in an environment that is already fun and pleasant already".

Q4. Do you believe the spiritual aspect of AA is wrong?

A4. Absolutely not actually I think it probably makes a significant impact on those that truly embrace it. The problem is a lot of people will start running as soon as they get a hint of religion and or spirituality. It smacks too much of a cult and allows the ego to instantly come up with a thousand reasons why the process won't work.

While I am not religious you will be quickly be able to gather from a quick Google search of my other books that I am very spiritual minded. I face most challenges in my life with a specific spiritual technique called Ho'oponopono. I choose not to refer to it in the book until now for the very reasons stated above.

Ho'oponopono is the ancient Hawaiian spiritual process of acceptance, forgiveness and gratitude. Rosario Montenegro offers one of the most concise stories of how Dr Hew Len brought this amazing tradition into popular modern culture around the world.

More than thirty years ago, in Hawaii, at the Hawaii State Hospital, there was a special ward, a clinic for the mentally ill criminals. People who had committed extremely serious crimes were assigned there either because they had a very deep mental disorder or because they needed to be checked to see if they were sane enough to stand trial. They had committed murder, rape, kidnapping or other such crimes. According to a nurse that worked there in those years, the place was so bleak that not even the paint could stick to the walls; everything was decaying, terrifying, repulsive. No day would pass without a patient-inmate attacking another inmate or a member of the staff.

The people working there were so frightened that they would walk close to the walls if they saw an inmate coming their way in a corridor, even though they were all shackled, all the time. The inmates would never be brought outside to get fresh air because of their relentlessly threatening attitude. The scarcity of staff was a chronic occurrence. Nurses, wardens, and employees would prefer to be on sick-leave most of the time in order not to confront such a depressive and dangerous environment.

One day, a newly appointed clinical psychologist, a Dr. Stanley Hew Len, arrived at the ward. The nurses rolled their eyes, bracing themselves for one more guy that was going to bug them with new theories and proposals to fix the horrid situation, who would walk away as soon as things became unpleasant, around a month later, usually.

However, this new doctor wouldn't do anything like that. Actually, he didn't seem to be doing anything in particular, except just coming in and always being cheerful and smiling, in a very natural, relaxed way. He wasn't even particularly early in arriving every morning. From time to time he would ask for the files of the inmates.

He never tried to see them personally, though. Apparently he just sat in an office, looked at their files, and to members of the staff who showed an interest he would tell them about a weird thing called Ho'oponopono. Little by little things started to change in the hospital. One day somebody would try again to paint those walls and they actually stayed painted, making the environment more palatable. The gardens started being taken care of, some tennis courts were repaired and some prisoners that up until then would never be allowed to go outside started playing tennis with the staff. Other prisoners would be allowed out of their shackles, or would receive less heavy pharmacological drugs. More and more obtained permission to go outside, unshackled, without causing trouble to the hospital's employees.

In the end, the atmosphere changed so much that the staff was not on sick leave any more. Actually, more people than were needed now go to work there. Prisoners gradually started to be released. Dr. Hew Len worked there close to four years. In the end, there remained only a couple of inmates that were eventually relocated elsewhere, and the clinic for the mentally insane criminals had to close.

Simply put, Ho'oponopono is based on the knowledge that anything that happens to you or that you perceive, the entire world where you live is your own creation and thus, it is entirely your responsibility.

☐ *Your boss is a tyrant? It's your responsibility.*
☐ *Your children are not good students? It's your responsibility.*

- *There are wars and you feel bad because you are a good person, a pacifist? The war is your responsibility.*
- *You see that children around the world are hungry and malnourished if not starving? Their want is your responsibility.*

No exceptions. Literally, the world is your world, it is your creation. As Dr. Hew Len points out: didn't you notice that whenever you experience a problem, you are there?

It's your responsibility, doesn't mean it's your fault, it means that you are responsible for healing yourself in order to heal whatever or whoever it is that appears to you as a problem.

It might sound crazy, or just plain metaphorical, that the world is your creation. But if you look carefully, you will realize that whatever you call the world and perceive as the world is your world, it is the projection of your own mind.

If you go to a party you can see how in the same place, with the same light, the same people, the same food, drink, music and atmosphere, some will enjoy themselves while others will be bored, some will be overenthusiastic and some depressed, some will be talkative and others will be silent.

The "out there" for every one of them seems the same, but if one were to connect their brains to machines, immediately it would show how different areas of the brain would come alive, how different perceptions there are from one person to the next. So even if they apparently share it, the "out there" is not the same for them, let alone their inner world, their emotions.

How can you use Ho'oponopono to help with giving up drinking?

Three steps: by recognizing that whatever comes to you is your creation, the outcome of bad memories buried in your mind; by regretting whatever errors of body, speech and mind caused those bad memories, and by requesting divine Intelligence within yourself to release those memories, to set you free. Then, of course, you say thank you.

There are seminars where they teach you many tricks to help this process, but according to Joe Vitale, Dr. Hew Len himself uses the simplest of the formulas from Ho'oponopono. Whenever a matter arises –and they arise incessantly– addressing the Divine within you, you only have to say: I'm sorry, Please forgive me, Thank You, I Love you.

If you want to discover more about the origins and evidence of Ho'oponopono, look out for a book by Joe Vitale called Zero Limits. Joe goes into great detail about how this amazing principle that has been passed down the ages literally creates miracles.

Q5. I have stopped drinking and I am really happy about that but I dream about alcohol every night. Is this normal and how do I stop it?

A5. Yes it is completely normal and sometimes the dreams will be so vivid and detailed that you will wake up completely convinced that you had been drinking during the night.

I remember when I first stopped I had a dream where I was knocking back shot after shot of neat whiskey. The dream was so lucid that when I awoke I emptied every garbage bin in the house to make sure there were no empty bottles there. I think I dreamed about drinking for a week solid before they started to slow down. For the first few months of my sobriety, I would have a drinking dream about once a week and now it is down to about once a year. Although they still take me by surprise when they happen and I wake thinking 'what the heck was that all about'!

As to why this strange phenomenon happens is up for debate. Personally I believe that it is due to a combination of reasons. Firstly your dreams are a way for your brain to filter and sort the information you have absorbed during the day. Your brain files away important information and discards the junk. When you first stop drinking you are acutely aware of not having a drink in your hand and you are constantly reminded of situations where before you would have consumed alcohol. As alcohol is still playing an active role in your life, albeit by its absence it is still considered worthy of processing by your subconscious mind. As you stop noticing the nonappearance of alcohol in your day-to-day life it will appear less in your dreams accordingly.

The second reason for alcohol dreams is down to a change in brain chemistry. Back when I was drinking I would rarely manage to get past 8pm, I would drink a bottle or two of wine and would stumble upstairs to crash into bed – often even before my children's bedtime. I would blink my bloodshot eyes open ten hours later but I would feel like I had had only about an hours sleep. This is because alcohol is a mild anesthetic and despite what the doctor tells you before an operation anesthesia does not cause sleep but rather a reversible coma.

When you are under general anesthetic it is not possible to dream because brain activity is slowed to virtually nothing. Dreams are complex and creative actions of the brain and the chemical is preventing anything but the basic functions to support life.

None of the self-repair and cell regeneration happens during this time, as the brain cannot coordinate the process. When you awake from a drunken 'sleep' perhaps less than half the night you weren't sleeping at all but rather in an anesthetic induced coma.

When you have been drinking heavily for a long period of time the brain and body get used to having this chemical permanently pumping around the system. Stopping drinking is like driving around for year with the parking break on the entire time and then suddenly taking if off. When you stop drinking suddenly the brain has to get used to operating without the breaks on.

The absence of alcohol in the brain is an unusual and significant event that the subconscious has to get its head around (excuse the pun). So it is understandable that this focus would leak into our dreams. Don't worry; perhaps the single biggest reason human beings are at the top of the food chain is our ability to adapt. Within weeks these dreams will slow and fade away.

Got a question? Ask me live in my online stop drinking club at www.StopDrinkingExpert.com

Chapter Fourteen
Subconscious Reprogramming

The final step in the 'Alcohol Lied to Me' method is subconscious reprogramming. As we have discussed, all the issues we face in life are our responsibility, as they are manifest directly by us, via the programs that run in our subconscious mind. Most of these sub-routines are beneficial and serve a valuable purpose such as controlling our body temperature and keeping us breathing at the correct rate. However, along our journey through this life we pick up the odd erroneous program that creates unhelpful manifestations. These 'bad programs' make us fat, create low self-esteem and even get us addicted to harmful substances.

Thankfully we are prevented by nature from lifting the hood on the subconscious mind and tinkering with the engine. Of course our ego would have us believe that we are master mechanics, fully capable of making perfect adjustments to this most powerful of computers. The subconscious knows better and the gate is kept firmly closed to the over zealous ego.

Using hypnosis we can bypass the conscious mind and implant positive corrections directly into the subconscious. As this part of the mind has no ability to judge or question, the implanted commands are run exactly as requested.

This section of the method is optional and many have stopped drinking completely without ever having used one of my hypnosis downloads. However, as with everything else I have told you so far. This was an important element for me and I want you to use every tool in the box to ensure we get the job done in one painless motion. If you do think these powerful audio tracks would help you then please stop by my website for the mp3 download details.

It is important that we ensure we fully understand what hypnosis is, or more importantly what it is not. Hypnosis is not black magic, a party trick nor a piece of theatre. It is a naturally occurring process of the brain that has unfortunately attracted some seriously bad press over recent years; some might say even OJ Simpson has had better press than hypnosis! Thankfully, for over two thousand years it was documented and practiced with a great deal of respect. How bizarre that this long studied and amazing action of the human mind was essentially defamed by a man in a bar trying to convince girls to remove their clothes.

The traditional stage hypnotist is considered by most right thinking hypnotherapists and psychologists as a blundering incompetent dabbling in something they don't truly understand. If they did understand the amazing process they are playing with, I would suggest they would find something more productive to do with it than make a person believe they are a little fluffy duck called Roger!

A common misconception about hypnosis is that it is sleep. Although a hypnotized person appears to be sleeping, they are actually quite alert. Hypnosis is very difficult to describe, as nobody actually knows what is going on inside the mind of a subject. What we do know is that while in the trance state, the subject becomes very suggestible. A subject's attention, while they are going into trance, is narrowed down gradually.

Many areas of normal communication are removed one by one. Starting with sight, a person is asked to close his eyes and concentrate. Other senses are then removed from the equation; some people even lose complete feeling of their body. That may sound frightening, but it is accomplished in a slow, pleasant way, rather than suddenly turning off of a switch.

You enter a world of hyper relaxation and at the same time hyper awareness. As you might expect, as you remove certain senses the remaining ones become more acute to compensate. Often people who have been under hypnosis will come around and claim "it did not work". When you enquire as to why they believe hypnosis did not occur, they make statements such as "I could hear everything", "I could even hear the cars going past the window!" This is all part of the misconception that hypnosis is sleep, and that during trance you are unconscious, when in actual fact you are hyper conscious.

I am telling you about hypnosis not because I want you to take to the stage, but because I want you to understand the truly amazing power of the subconscious mind. A person in hypnosis is highly suggestible. The hypnotist has direct access to the person's subconscious without having to go through the conscious mind. This is how they can convince a six foot tall, 18 stone man he is a light gentle ballet dancer and have him pirouetting his way around the stage.

Hypnosis is so natural, that you do it dozens of times a day without even realizing it. Have you ever driven home at the end of your working day and arrived home with no memory of the journey? Hypnosis just paid you a visit, your brain was using the opportunity of this familiar and fairly simple task to filter and file information in your brain.

You may notice yourself at work blankly staring at the computer screen in a deep peaceful daydream. This happens due to the vast amount of information constantly entering your brain, every few hours your mind must pause a little to filter and file all the information you have learned. Placing it in the correct storage area of the brain.

For example, let's say in the last hour your brain has learned that the color of the walls in the canteen are yellow. It has also learnt that your new managers' name is David. It must ensure the information you will need on an on going basis is stored close to hand. Unfortunately this is at the expense of the canteen walls, and I am sorry to say, if questioned, you may have trouble remembering what color those walls were - but who cares, walls may have ears, but I have noticed they stay pretty dumb when asked for a pay rise!

If you are interested in studying the power of hypnosis to a greater extent, I would suggest you read a book called 'Patterns of the Hypnotic Techniques of Milton H. Erickson', by John Grinder.

In my online stop drinking club, I use hypnosis to further embed the six steps of my stop drinking method. I do this because I know that the conscious mind is a guard dog. The sort of animal the mail man must first distract before he opens the gate and creeps up the path to post the mail through the letterbox, after doing so he sneaks back out, hopefully without being noticed. During this book I have been directly talking to your guard dog, you can choose to accept what I am saying, or dismiss it. During hypnosis you do not have that problem; all suggestions are accepted without judgment because the words are directed to the subconscious.

Don't lie there waiting for something magical to happen, don't expect or demand anything, you will also need to be prepared to catch your ego trying to pull you out of the moment. It's fine when it does, if you find your mind wandering just notice what has happened, smile and refocus on the now. Relax and let the music and my words drift over you. There is nothing that you can do wrong, free yourself of that concern and let go of all expectation.

Part of the fear of giving up drinking is that you might spend the rest of your life with an itch you can't scratch; Living in a permanent state of wanting a drink but not being able to touch it. This is not a cure; this is a torturous and constant battle with the ego that you can't possibly expect to win in the long term. Imagine being so at ease with alcohol that you can honestly say you don't want a drink, you don't like the taste of it, and if someone pushed a glass of it into your hand you would rather go out of your way to find a replacement than take the slightest sip. This state is possible, I know because I have been through the process I have just described to you, and now I live it everyday.

As I close this book I will share with you one final observation from the point of view of an ex-drinker. Yesterday I was a guest at a wedding set in a beautiful castle in the North East of England. Everything was perfect, the groom and his ushers were dressed in smart dark grey suits complete with gloves and top hats. The bride looked stunning in a tight fitting cream bodice and flowing gown.

As the bride walked down the aisle on the arm of her proud father, you could see that she was trembling with nerves and anticipation. As she recited the lines of the marriage ceremony, her voice quivered and the gathered audience of family and friends made sympathetic and encouraging eyes at her.

At the end of the service as friends gathered around the happy couple, I was bemused to watch on as the wedding organizer pushed a massive glass of neat whiskey into the bride's hand as though he was a doctor administering a vital antidote.

"Forget the Champagne love, I think it's time for something a bit stronger", he said as he encouraged the bride to take a big gulp. The bride smiled and thanked him profusely.

Excuse me! Why... at the happiness moment of your life to date, in the precise moment that you had planned and prepared for over several years. In this moment, where all your dreams come true, why would anyone in their right mind knowingly gulp down an anesthetic that dulls their ability to experience reality? It's like planning a dream vacation, saving up the money to go, traveling thousands of miles to get there and then as soon as you step off the airplane pulling on a blindfold and sticking your fingers in your ears.

There is no situation where alcohol makes our experience better. These days no matter what life throws at me, from the joyful celebration of a party with friends or the pain and grief that comes at the loss of a loved one. I am grateful that I don't need or want alcohol to further complicate the situation. No matter how bad it gets, I know that alcohol can only make it worse, and that is a truly liberating feeling indeed.

Thank you for reading 'Alcohol Lied to Me', I hope it has the same profound and dramatic effect on your life that it had on mine. I do hope you take the next step toward a life in control of alcohol and join my exclusive online membership club at www.StopDrinkingExpert.com

If you have enjoyed this book I am sure you won't mind obliging me with a small favor. The effectiveness of my work is vitally important to me, and I would encourage you to rate and review this book wherever you bought it from. If you believe the concepts we have talked about in 'Alcohol Lied to Me' will be of benefit to you, would you please help spread the word and give this book a 5 star rating that reflects your honest opinion.

Recommended links

- ☐ www.craigbeck.com :
- ☐ www.StopDrinkingExpert.com :

Other products by Craig Beck

252 lbs   192 lbs

Craig Beck is one of the fittest and healthiest people you will ever meet. So why is he known around the world as 'Fat Guy Friday'?

In truth, that's exactly what he used to be.. a big fat guy! Until one day he said enough is enough and broke the cycle of yo-yo dieting that had plagued his life. On Friday 10th September 2010, he stood on the scales at a depressing 252lbs. He was the heaviest he had ever been in his life, something as simple as walking up a flight of stairs would leave him gasping for air, he struggled to play games with his children, and was the most miserable he had ever been.

A former hypnotist, Craig knew that all problems in life are primarily the result of dysfunctional programs running in the subconscious mind, which are creating the very things we are unhappy with. Whilst he was building a system to deal with his own ever-expanding waistline, he discovered two common traits shared by virtually all overweight people.

By removing these two secret problems, he found that no matter who tried his system, they lost weight. Better than that, at no point did any of them report being hungry or irritable during the process. In Fat Guy Friday, Craig pulls no punches and delivers a wake up call designed to change your life for the better, forever!

• The two reasons why you are overweight.

• Why every diet you have ever tried has failed.

• What the diet industry doesn't want you to know.

• The secrets only slim people know.

• How to lose weight and feel great without feeling hungry, ever!

• Feel better and more healthy than you ever thought possible.

Join the Fat Guy Friday Club today and discover why the traditional low fat diet is keeping you fat. Actually, it's as illogical as trying to extinguish a fire by throwing gasoline on it. Sure, it's wet like water, but you will end up with the opposite of what you wanted!

THE TRUTH: The low fat diet you thought was helping you lose weight is actually making you fatter and more miserable than you thought possible - join the club today and discover the secrets the dieting industry doesn't want you to know!

www.FatGuyFriday.com

The Alcohol Illusion by Craig Beck

Alcohol is a drug that has achieved the ultimate illusion. It has managed to convince the western world that it isn't a drug at all, but rather a harmless social pleasantry.

A product that does none of the things that the marketing promises and yet remains unchallenged for making such false claims.

A beverage that kills over 2,500,000 people a year and yet still remains legal in virtually every country around the world.

Craig Beck is known as the Stop Drinking Expert because he helps people to see the truth about alcohol, hidden behind the smoke and mirrors of the marketing and our own self created social conditioning. His book Alcohol Lied to Me has topped bestseller charts for many years and has been translated into several different languages.

"Alcohol is the ultimate wolf in sheep's clothing, a deeply insidious and dangerous drug packaged into pretty bottles and marketed as a fun, social pleasantry by the drinks manufacturers. The western world is conditioned from birth to believe that good times and alcohol go hand in hand.

In reality consuming this drug is like playing a very dangerous game of Buckaroo, the longer you keep playing the more chance you have the mule will kick and destroy your world.", Craig Beck

In The Alcohol Illusion Craig gives away the secrets of the magician and helps you see how the drug traps you and keeps you locked in a never ending loop. Once you see how the trick is done… escape is only a matter of time.

www.StopDrinkingExpert.com

Made in the USA
Middletown, DE
05 October 2015